CLAIRE BENTON-EVANS

A Year's Worth of Instant Bible
Assemblies for Primary Schools

www.kevinmayhew.com

First published in Great Britain in 2013 by Kevin Mayhew Ltd
Buxhall, Stowmarket, Suffolk IP14 3BW
Tel: +44 (0) 1449 737978 Fax: +44 (0) 1449 737834
E-mail: info@kevinmayhewltd.com

www.kevinmayhew.com

© Copyright 2013 Claire Benton-Evans.

The right of Claire Benton-Evans to be identified as the author of this work has been asserted by her in accordance with the Copyright, Designs and Patents Act 1988.

The publishers wish to thank all those who have given their permission to reproduce copyright material in this publication.

Every effort has been made to trace the owners of copyright material and we hope that no copyright has been infringed. Pardon is sought and apology made if the contrary be the case, and a correction will be made in any reprint of this book.

All rights reserved. No part of this publication may be reproduced, stored in a retrieval system, or transmitted, in any form or by any means, electronic, mechanical, photocopying, recording, or otherwise, without the prior written permission of the publisher.

Unless stated otherwise, Scripture quotations are taken from *The New Revised Standard Version of the Bible*, copyright © 1989 Division of Christian Education of the National Council of the Churches of Christ in the USA. Used by permission. All rights reserved.

ISBN 978 1 84867 675 6
Catalogue No. 1501416

Cover design by Rob Mortonson
© Images used under licence from Shutterstock Inc.
Edited by Nicki Copeland
Typeset by Richard Weaver

Printed and bound in Great Britain

Contents

About the author   5

Introduction   7

Big Bang – The Creation story   9

Rain, Rain, Go Away! – Noah's Ark   12

The Great Babble – The Tower of Babel   16

The Long Wait – God keeps his promise to Abraham and Sarah   20

Two Brothers – Isaac and Ishmael   23

The Big Fight – Jacob wrestles with an angel   26

The Dreamer – Joseph's colourful life   30

Blood, Bugs and Boils – The Ten Plagues of Egypt   35

The Great Escape – The Crossing of the Red Sea   39

The Giant – David and Goliath   43

'QUAKE! WIND! FIRE! – The prophet Elijah meets God in the desert   47

Staying Alive – God saves three men from the fiery furnace   51

Teeth and Claws – Daniel in the lions' den   55

Eaten Alive! – Jonah and the Big Fish   58

Locusts and Honey – The story of John the Baptist and Advent   62

The New Baby – The Christmas story   66

Missing! – Mary and Joseph lose Jesus   69

Wet, Wet, Wet – The story of Jesus' baptism   73

Deserted – Jesus in the wilderness and the start of Lent   76

Gone Fishing – Jesus calls the disciples   79

The Miracle Drink – Jesus turns water into wine   83

The All-You-Can-Eat Picnic – Jesus feeds the five thousand   87

In Charge – Jesus heals the centurion's servant   90

Get Up! – Jesus heals the paralysed man   94

Wake Up! – Jesus brings Lazarus back from the dead   97

Man Overboard! – Jesus walks on the waves   100

Take Care – The parable of the Good Samaritan   104

Lost and Found – The parable of the prodigal son   108

It's Not Fair! – The parable of the workers in the vineyard   112

Seeds, Weeds and Stones – The parable of the sower   116

A Tale of Two Sisters – Martha and Mary   120

Dazzled! – the story of Jesus' Transfiguration   124

Smelly Feet – Jesus washes his disciples' feet   127

Crucify Him! – The story of Good Friday   131
He's Alive! – The story of Easter Day   134
I Don't Believe It! – The story of Doubting Thomas   138
Come and Have Breakfast! – Jesus appears to the disciples on the beach   142
Goodbye – Jesus ascends into heaven   145
Wind and Fire – The story of Pentecost, the Church's birthday   149

About the author

Claire Benton-Evans writes exclusively for Kevin Mayhew and now leads popular workshops on prayer and storytelling for churches across the UK. She provides schools' INSET training in children's spirituality and as the author of *Beastly Bible Stories*, she enjoys visiting schools with her new *Beastly Bible Stories Schools Event*.

Claire studied at Oxford before teaching English and Drama in London, North Devon and Cornwall. She lives with her husband and three children in the Scottish Borders, where she works as the Youth and Children Officer for the Diocese of Edinburgh.

Details of Claire's other titles and information about her training and workshops can be found on her website at www.clairebentonevans.com or visit www.kevinmayhew.com.

Introduction

Bible stories are an essential part of education, for children of all faiths and none. References to this shared cultural heritage are everywhere, and children are poorer for not understanding them: for example, when they help an injured friend to the school nurse and are praised for being a 'good Samaritan'; when a football commentator describes a certain F.A. Cup match as a 'David and Goliath' contest or when they wonder why a *Doctor Who* episode about rejuvenation is called 'The Lazarus Experiment'. This book, as the title suggests, is concerned with telling these stories, drawn from both the Old and the New Testaments. There is an assembly for each of the 39 weeks of the school year, which retells an important Bible story in a fresh, accessible and memorable way. Each story makes a brief point – a short 'thought to take away' – and this is explained both in terms of what the story means to Christians and the general lesson that everyone might draw from it. For ease of reference, the plot and the point are summarised at the beginning of each story. Each assembly also includes an interactive prayer and music suggestions.

This book is intended to be as **user-friendly** as possible. The assemblies are designed to be instantly deliverable by busy head teachers, by multi-tasking clergy and, at the last minute, by any teacher in a school whose assembly speaker has failed to arrive. They can be read straight off the page, with no preparation. For those who have the time and inclination, there are some suggestions for possible uses of IT and props which may enhance the storytelling, but these are strictly optional.

Most importantly, all these assemblies are **resource-free**. Dramatic Bible storytelling in schools – from *Open the Book* to the annual Nativity play – usually requires costumes, props, a script and rehearsal. These things are well worth doing, but they demand time and resources. By contrast, the storytelling in this book does not require any costumes or kit, and instead makes the most of a school's greatest existing resources: children and their imaginations. All these stories require active audience participation: from their opening shout of 'What's the story?' onwards, children will be asked to use their hands, feet and voices to contribute to the storytelling. Often they will be invited to close their eyes and picture themselves in a scene, because these tales from desert lands are a world away from a school assembly hall on a rainy Tuesday morning, and they require an imaginative leap. Sometimes a few confident volunteers are invited to take part in the story as it is told. In my experience of teaching drama to all ages, Primary school children can be fearless and creative improvisers: they take suggestions and run with them, and can be far less self-conscious than teenagers or adults. If, for example, you ask your volunteers to be lost and thirsty in the desert, you will usually get plenty of dramatic trudging, brow-mopping, staggering and throat-clutching.

All these interactive elements are designed to make these stories fun to tell and entertaining to hear. They hold children's attention, making them wonder what they will be asked to do next. So invite the children in your school to shout, 'What's the story?' They shouldn't need too much encouragement to make a noise! Then simply turn the page and tell the story together.

Big Bang
The Creation story

The Plot
God makes the world in six days flat. This is an ancient story that describes in simple terms what we now know about the Big Bang and evolution: something came out of nothing and evolved over millions of years into the world (and the universe) we know today.

(Genesis 1:1–2:3)

The Point
God gave us this world containing everything we need. Our job is to look after it.

Story

I've got a story for you today. If you want to hear it, shout, 'What's the story?'

Encourage all to shout: **What's the story?**

This story is about how the world began. It is called *(pause, then very loudly)* 'BIG BANG!' In the beginning there was nothing at all. No light, no dark, no up, no down, no yesterday, today or tomorrow. Then God said, 'Let there be light.' He gave the order and it kicked off the whole of creation, so he must have spoken in a very powerful way. Can you imagine God giving that order? Let's all use our biggest, strongest voices and shout together, 'Let there be light!'

After a count of three, all shout: **Let there be light!**

And – BIG BANG! There was light. So that made Day and Night – Day One. But God was just getting started. He spread a big dome over this watery planet and he called it Sky. Can you use your hands as if you're spreading out the sky?

Spread your hands above your head as if smoothing out a canopy, and encourage the children to do the same.

There you go – Day Two: Sky. Now on Day Three, God really got going. Does anyone know what he made next?

Invite suggestions.

WHAT'S THE STORY?

God heaped up the dry land and called it Earth; then he scooped out deep channels for the waters and called them Seas. Then out of the earth God called the grass and the trees and everything green. Now, I'd like you all to think of a plant, flower or tree. I'm thinking of an oak tree – what about you?

Invite some children to say what they are thinking of, then ask everyone to shout out together the name of a plant, flower or tree after a count of three.

What a lot of green, growing things! So that was Day Three. Then God lit up the sky. He started with a ball of fire – the sun. Can you all stretch your arms in the air like the white-hot rays of the sun?

Everyone stretches their arms.

Then God made the cool, white moon. Can you cup your hands together like a crescent moon?

Everyone cups their hands, pressing the inside of the wrists together, and tilts them to one side to look like a crescent.

And finally God made the stars. Can you make your hands twinkle like stars?

Everyone opens and closes their hands to make starburst shapes.

And God was only on Day Four! On Day Five, things got noisy. God gave the go-ahead for everything that swims and everything that flies. Dogfish! Dolphins! Crocodiles! Crows! Pterodactyls! Parrots! Imagine the noise and the mess as shoals, pods and flocks moved in. Can you make a noise like one of those creatures? You could whistle like a dolphin, sing like a whale, chirp like a robin or squawk like a crow. Let's make some noise like all those swimming, flying creatures!

Everyone makes their chosen noise until you signal for them to stop.

On Day Six, God turned to the earth and brought it to life with all kinds of animals: worms and wombats; earwigs and elephants; termites, tabby cats and *Tyrannosaurus Rex*. Can you make a noise like your favourite animal?

Everyone makes their chosen noise until you signal for them to stop.

God knew he'd done a good job – but it wasn't quite finished. He needed somebody to look after this beautiful, messy, evolving world he had created, so he made the first two human beings, called Adam and Eve. He gave them the world and said, 'This is ALL for you. Look after it.' Then God knew he'd done a very good job, so at the end of that first week he had a day off and he rested all day long.

BIG BANG – THE CREATION STORY

The Point

This very old story tells us in simple terms how God kick-started the whole of creation: he made something come out of nothing and evolve into the world we know today. The story reminds us that the world has everything in it that we need, and like Adam and Eve, it's our job to look after it. If you recycle your rubbish, care for a pet, turn off the light when you leave your bedroom, or walk to school whenever you can instead of coming by car, then you are helping to look after our wonderful world.

The Prayer

For our prayers today, we will take some time to notice the wonderful world we live in. I'd like you to sit for thirty seconds and use the time to listen and look. Can you see the sky? Can you see or hear the weather? Can you hear birds singing? Be really quiet and listen. Then look around you in this room, at the great variety of people here. Notice all the different colours of hair and eyes, and notice how cleverly your own body has been put together, with its strong bones, stretchy muscles and elastic skin. For thirty seconds, let's be quiet and notice how wonderfully we are made and how amazing this world is.

Pause for thirty seconds, then end the prayer with the following words.

God our Creator,
thank you for this wonderful world.
Help us to look after it all.
Amen.

Song

'Who put the colours in the rainbow?'

Plus

Suggestions for optional extras:

IT	Display a slideshow of pictures of our beautiful world, including sunsets, seas, mountains, trees, plants and creatures of all kinds.
PROPS	If this is a special Harvest assembly, the story could be illustrated by children holding up art work they have done in class, depicting the different aspects of creation. The prayer time could be marked by a sand timer.
MUSIC	'Thank you for the sun'[1]. You could also play 'What a Wonderful World' by Louis Armstrong as the children enter and leave the assembly.

---

1. Alison Carver, *Sing the day through*, Kevin Mayhew 2009.

Rain, Rain, Go Away!
Noah's Ark

The Plot

God sees his first people behaving badly and is sorry that he made them. He decides to destroy the earth with a flood. Noah is the exception: he's a good man who follows God's orders and builds an ark. The flood comes but Noah's family is saved, along with breeding pairs of every species. God promises that he will never again destroy the earth.

(Genesis 6:5–9:17)

The Point

Noah trusted God and so can we.

Story

I've got a story for you today. If you want to hear it, shout, 'What's the story?'

Encourage all to shout: **What's the story?**

This story is about a time when it rained for forty days and forty nights and the whole earth was flooded. It is called 'Rain, Rain, Go Away!' A long, long time ago, when the world was young, there lived a good man called Noah who believed in God. Can I have a volunteer to be Noah?

Bring Noah forward.

God was pleased with Noah, but he was sad because wherever he looked, everyone else was being bad: people were hurting each other and messing up their beautiful world, so God decided to wash the earth clean and start again. God wanted to save Noah, so he told him: 'You must build an enormous ark.'

Noah asked, 'What's that?'

God replied, 'It's a great big boat with enough room in it for all your family and for two of every kind of creature that lives on the earth. Make sure you take all sorts of food with you, too – enough for a long journey. Because I am going to make a great flood which will wash over the earth, and nothing and no one will survive it unless they are on your ark.'

So Noah did what God told him: he built a huge ark.

Invite your volunteer to pretend to hammer wood and build one side of his ark across the front of the assembly hall.

Then he invited all the creatures on earth to come into the ark! Now, that's all of you. Can you use your hands to make a creature? *(Demonstrate these actions with your hands and fingers as you describe them.)* You could give yourself big, flappy ears like an elephant; you could make wriggly legs like a spider; you could make your hand crawl along like a caterpillar; you could make big, round eyes like an owl. Decide what you're going to be and how you're going to use your hands to make your creature.

Allow a very short time for decisions and practice, which will be a bit noisy, then call for quiet.

Now, using ONLY OUR HANDS, not our voices, let's see all the animals that we have in our ark.

Everyone demonstrates their animal impressions for a short time.

What a wonderful collection of animals! Noah gathered them all into his ark and closed the doors. *(Encourage Noah to mime doing this.)* When they were all safely on board, it began to rain.

Tap your fingers lightly on the floor or a chair and encourage everyone else to do so.

The rain got heavier *(drum your hands loudly)* and heavier *(drum loudly with your feet, again encouraging general participation)* until the earth was completely covered with water.

Encourage the drumming to continue for a short time and then make a signal to stop.

Finally, the rain stopped. Noah came out of his ark and looked to the north, south, east and west. He could see nothing but water! The ark sailed on for days, and then months, but no one ever shouted, 'Land ahoy!' At last Noah sent out a raven to look for dry land.

As you mention each bird, encourage Noah to use his hands together to mime a bird flapping away.

But the raven just kept looking and looking. So then Noah sent out a dove, but it couldn't find anywhere to land and came straight back to the ark. Noah waited, then sent out the dove again, and this time she came back with a fresh olive leaf in her beak. At last, Noah had proof that there was dry land somewhere, and before long the water disappeared and everyone left the ark – Noah and his family and all the animals. God told them all to spread out across the world and have families, so that his beautiful earth would be full of life once more.

Then God promised that he would never again destroy the earth. As a sign of his promise, he stretched a rainbow across the sky. Do you know the colours of the rainbow? *(say or sing)* 'Violet, indigo, blue and green, yellow, orange and red.'

WHAT'S THE STORY?

Encourage everyone to repeat this after you.

Let's have a round of applause for Noah and all his animals!

Everyone applauds and Noah sits down.

The Point

Noah trusted God. He must have had questions: 'Do I really need to build an ark? How am I going to get all these animals on board?' As the flood waters rose, he must have asked himself, 'Are we going to get out of this alive?' Yet Noah trusted God and lived to see God make a new promise with his creation. This story reminds us that we can trust God, too, because he's always on our side.

The Prayer

For our prayers today, we will use our hands to make the shape of a dove.

Encourage everyone to curl their thumbs together and flap their hands like wings.

This is like the dove that brought Noah the olive leaf. It was the sign he'd been hoping for: it proved the flood was over. This dove is a reminder that we always have hope, and we can always trust in God. Whenever you're worried or scared, like Noah and the animals were in the flood, remember this dove, then put your hands together and pray.

Flap your hands like a dove's wings then bring them together in prayer. Encourage everyone to do the same.

Then say this simple prayer. It goes like this:

God who made me, *(encourage everyone to repeat this and the following lines after you)*
please look after me and the people I love.
Amen.

With our hands together, let us pray:
God who made me,
please look after me and the people I love.
Amen.

Song

'It's a great, great world'[2]

---

2. Alison Carver, *30 Catchy New Assembly Songs*, Kevin Mayhew 2009.

Plus

Suggestions for optional extras:

IT A slideshow of pictures of rain and stormy seas.

PROPS A long strip of blue fabric to represent the flood waters, to be waved by volunteers.

MUSIC 'Think of a world without any flowers'[3]

---

3. *Anglican Hymns Old & New*, Kevin Mayhew 2008.

The Great Babble
The Tower of Babel

The Plot
The earliest people are all living in one place and speaking the same language. They work together to build a tower up to heaven, but God worries that they are becoming unstoppable, so he mixes up their language and scatters them all over the world. They leave their tower unfinished and the place is named Babel because of the babble of different languages.

(Genesis 11:1-9)

The Point
We are all different, but if we can understand each other, anything's possible.

Story

I've got a story for you today. If you want to hear it, shout, 'What's the story?'

Encourage all to shout: **What's the story?**

This story starts quietly but it ends with a big noisy argument: it's called 'The Great Babble.' Once upon a time, not long after the world began, all the people on earth spoke the same language. They used the same words. Together they settled on a piece of land and made plans. 'Let's make ourselves some bricks,' they said. They agreed and they shook each other's hands. Can you turn to the person on your right, shake their hand and say 'OK'?

Encourage everyone to shake their neighbour's hand and say: **OK.**

So the people made lots and lots of bricks. Can I have some volunteers to help me?

Line up your volunteers and give them a simple, repetitive mime to perform: shaping clay into bricks.

Everyone worked well together until they had made an enormous pile of bricks.

Encourage your volunteers to give each other a 'high five' to mark their achievement.

THE GREAT BABBLE – THE TOWER OF BABEL

Then they said, 'Let's build ourselves a city, and finish it with a tower that reaches right up to heaven. Then we'll be famous. We'll be one big family and we won't be scattered to the ends of the earth.' Everyone agreed this was a great plan so they shook each other's hands. Now turn to the person on your left, shake their hand and say 'Great plan!'

Encourage everyone to shake their neighbour's hand and say: **Great plan!**

So the people worked together to build the city, and they built the tallest tower the world had ever seen.

Encourage your volunteers to mime building a tall tower.

But God looked down from heaven and saw what the people were doing. He said, 'They are one people and they speak the same language, and look what they've managed to do together. This is only the beginning: now nothing will be impossible for them. I can't have that.' So God went down and mixed up their language so that it became many different languages, and he scattered the people to the ends of the earth.

Ask your volunteers to return to their places.

Then the people were confused. They used different words and they couldn't understand each other. When one man said, 'Where's my spade?' his friend said, 'Qué?' (*'kay'*) which means 'What?' in Spanish. Can everyone who has blond hair say 'Qué?'

Encourage everyone who has blond hair say: **Qué?**

Then her friend said 'Was?' (*'Vass'*) which means 'What?' in German. Can everyone who wears glasses say 'Was?'

Encourage everyone who wears glasses to say: **Was?**

The next person said 'Qu'est-ce que c'est?' (*'kess-kuh-say'*) which means 'What is it?' in French. Can everyone who has brown eyes say 'Qu'est-ce que c'est?'

Encourage everyone who has brown eyes to say: **Qu'est-ce que c'est?**

The next person said 'Quid dicis?' (*quid dee-kiss*) which means 'What are you saying?' in Latin. Can everyone who is sitting on the floor say 'Quid dicis?'

Encourage everyone who is sitting on the floor to say: **Quid dicis?**

The next person said πως λεγεις (*'pose leg-ace'*) which means 'What are you saying?' in Greek. Can everyone who is sitting on chairs say πως λεγεις (*'pose leg-ace'*)?

Encourage everyone who is sitting on chairs to say: **Pose leg-ace?**

Does anyone know how to say 'What?' in any other language?

WHAT'S THE STORY?

> *Invite suggestions.*

So this was the scene in our story: suddenly all those people who had understood each other perfectly found themselves speaking all these different languages and more. We are going to recreate this moment in the story. I'd like you to choose one of the words meaning 'What?' that we've heard today: it could be 'Qué?' or 'Was?' or 'Qu'est-ce que c'est?' or 'Quid dicis?' or πως λεγεις (*pose leg-ace*) or any other phrases you know. We're going to look confused, like the people in our story, and say this to each other over and over again until I raise my hand like this. So after a count of three, we'll each turn to our neighbour and say 'What?' in different languages.

> *Count to three and let the noise build until you signal for it to stop.*

What a noise! There was a great babble of voices like this in our story, and it got worse as the people misunderstood each other: they couldn't agree, and they wouldn't work together, so in the end the city and the tower were left unfinished. Ever since, the place has been known as Babble, or Babel.

The Point

This very old story of the tower of Babel tries to explain simply why different languages are spoken all over the world. But do you remember what God said at the start, when he saw people speaking the same language and understanding each other? He said, 'This is only the beginning: now nothing will be impossible for them.' We need to try and understand people who are different from us, whether they speak a different language or have different ways of doing things. If we don't try to understand each other, we'll end up arguing like the people in our story. But if we do manage to understand each other, then anything is possible!

The Prayer

For our prayer today, we'll use another language: sign language. This is the American Sign Language sign for 'I love you':

> *Demonstrate the sign, explaining the letters as you make them: with an upright clenched fist, palm forward, extend your index finger ('I') then your thumb (with the index finger this makes 'L' for 'love') and then your little finger (with the index finger and hand this make 'Y' for 'you').*

Now we will be quiet for a moment as we make the 'I love you' sign. Let's think about the people we love and as we do so, let's pray that we will learn to love each other, whatever our differences are.

> *Pause for a moment as everyone makes the sign.*

God of love,
help us to understand and love each other.
Amen.

Song

'I like red, you like blue'[4]

> **Plus**
>
> *Suggestions for optional extras:*
>
> **MUSIC**   'Do you know?'[5]

---

4. Barry Hart, *30 Catchy New Assembly Songs*, Kevin Mayhew 2009
5. Becky & Andy Silver, *Sing the day through*, Kevin Mayhew 2009.

The Long Wait
God keeps his promise to Abraham and Sarah

The Plot

God promises to make Abram the father of his chosen people – but he's an old, childless man. Twenty-four years later, Abram's son Isaac is born and God's promise is fulfilled. Abram is renamed Abraham, which means 'father of many nations'.

(Genesis 15–18:15, 21:1-7)

The Point

God keeps his promises in the end.

Story

I've got a story for you today. If you want to hear it, shout, 'What's the story?'

Encourage all to shout: **What's the story?**

This story is called 'The Long Wait'. Hands up if you find waiting difficult! When it's weeks or months until your birthday, hands up if you think 'I just can't wait!'

Encourage responses.

Well, this story is about a man who was very patient because he had to wait a very long time indeed. His name was Abram and he was specially chosen by God. Eventually, he became Abraham, the father of God's people. This is what happened.

One night, God spoke to Abram. He said, 'Don't be frightened, Abram. I will always look after you. You'll have a big reward.'

But Abram said, 'Like what? The only thing I want is a son, and I still haven't got any children. My servant's child will get everything when I die.

Then God said, 'No, he won't. You'll have children of your own. Look at the stars.'

Invite everyone to hold up their hands like stars.

God asked Abram to count the stars. Can you count all these stars we've made with our hands?

Encourage children to look around and try to count the hands.

THE LONG WAIT – GOD KEEPS HIS PROMISE TO ABRAHAM AND SARAH

Now imagine that each finger and thumb is a star! How many of those can you see?

Encourage children to look around and try to count the fingers and thumbs, then put their hands down.

There are too many for us to count! Well, Abram looked at the stars and he couldn't count them all. God said, 'You'll have as many people in your family as these stars. You will have so many descendants that you won't be able to count them all.' Abram believed God; and so God knew that he was a good man.

Now, the Bible often tells us how old people are: in today's story, Abram was 76 years old and his wife Sarai was 67. Who would like to be Abram and Sarai?

Invite two volunteers forward.

And now I need lots of volunteers to show us how old these two are.

Invite lots of volunteers forward and stand them in lines either side of Abram and Sarai.

We need 8 of you to line up next to Abram and hold up your fingers to show how old he is. That's 76 fingers!

Your volunteers together hold up 76 fingers.

Now we need 7 volunteers to do the same for Sarai: that's 67 fingers!

Your volunteers together hold up 67 fingers.

This is how old Abram and Sarai were when God promised them a great big family. That's quite an age to believe that you will still have children! Even so, Abram believed God. Sure enough, his first child, Ishmael, was born – 10 years later!

Invite up two more volunteers, one for each line. They each hold up 10 fingers, showing that Abram is 86 and Sarai is 77.

Ishmael was the son of Sarai's slave, Hagar. Sarai herself still longed for a child, although by then she was 77. Then, 13 years later, God told Abram that Sarai would give birth to their son, Isaac.

Invite up four more volunteers, two for each line. They hold up 13 fingers, showing that Abram is 99 and Sarai is 90.

He was 99 and she was 90! Even so, Abram still believed God, and Isaac was born a year later.

The last volunteers hold up one more finger.

WHAT'S THE STORY?

Abram, Isaac and Isaac's son, Jacob, became the fathers of the Jewish people. Abram was renamed 'Abraham', which means 'father of many', and Sarai was renamed Sarah, which means 'princess'. So God did keep his promises, although Abraham had to wait 24 years to see it happen, when he was 100 years old!

Applaud your volunteers and ask them to sit down.

The Point

We are used to things happening fast. If we search the Internet, Google gives us millions of results in a tenth of a second. God is different: he takes his own time, but he keeps his promises in the end. The story of Abraham and Sarah reminds us that, however long we wait, we can trust that God is on our side and he will never leave us on our own.

The Prayer

Abraham waited for 24 years for God to keep his promise. For our prayers today, we are going to practise waiting – for just 24 seconds. While we are waiting, we are going to pray for people who are waiting. You might know someone who is waiting for an operation, or who is waiting to move house, or who is waiting for an important letter or a really exciting treat. You might know about people in the news who are waiting to be helped or rescued. Let's be quiet and still for 24 seconds, while we pray for everyone who is waiting.

Pause for exactly 24 seconds.

God our Father,
please look after everyone who is waiting
and help them to trust in you.
Amen.

Song

'Father Abraham had many sons'[6]

Plus

Suggestions for optional extras:

IT   On a screen during the prayer, display a stop watch counting down 24 seconds.

PROPS   Head-cloths for Abram and Sarai and a beard for Abram.

MUSIC   'You can't always have what you want'[7]

---

6. Search the internet for lyrics and music; YouTube footage demonstrates the actions for this song.
7. Becky & Andy Silver, *Sing the day through*, Kevin Mayhew 2009.

Two Brothers
Isaac and Ishmael

The Plot

Abraham has two wives called Sarah and Hagar. They each have a son: Isaac and Ishmael. Isaac's mum, Sarah, is jealous of Hagar and her son, Ishmael. She makes Abraham send them both into the desert, but God looks after them. He promises that both boys will grow up to become the fathers of great nations. *(Genesis 21:8-21)*

The Point

The two brothers became fathers of two nations: Isaac's people are Jews and Ishmael's people are Muslims. Christians, Jews and Muslims all share the story of Abraham and his sons. It's a reminder that we share common ground.

Story

I've got a story for you today. If you want to hear it, shout, 'What's the story?'

Encourage all to shout: **What's the story?**

Today's story is called 'Two Brothers'. It comes from the beginning of the Bible and it's about two little boys for whom God had big plans. The two brothers became the fathers of Muslims and Jews, and their families live all over the world today.

This story begins in the desert. I want you to close your eyes and imagine that all around us is a big, hot, empty wilderness: there's nothing but sand and stones for miles and miles. We are sheltering from the burning sun in a big tent made of rugs and cloths. Outside there is a pool of clear water surrounded by a few trees which cast a little shade. You can hear laughing and running feet because two young boys are playing in and out of the tents. This is where our story starts. Can I have two volunteers to be the two boys?

Bring two volunteers forward and introduce them.

Their names were Isaac and Ishmael.

Encourage the volunteers to play 'Tag' back and forth at the front of the assembly hall.

They were used to playing and fighting together, as brothers do.

WHAT'S THE STORY?

Bring your volunteers back to stand by you.

Isaac's dad was Abraham and his mum was Sarah. He was their only son and they loved him very much. Ishmael's dad was Abraham, too, but his mum was a slave called Hagar. Abraham loved Ishmael, but Sarah was jealous of him. She hated to see the two boys playing together as equals, so she said to Abraham, 'Get rid of Ishmael and his mother!'

Abraham didn't want to lose his son, so he asked God what to do. God answered, 'Do as your wife says, but don't worry about your sons. They will both become fathers of great nations.' So Abraham took his son Isaac back into his tent *(ask Isaac to sit down)* and then he very sadly sent Ishmael into the desert with his mum. Can I have a volunteer to be Ishmael's mum, Hagar?

Bring forward an older child and ask your two volunteers to walk around (or up and down) the assembly hall, looking tired and hot as if they are in the desert.

Ishmael and Hagar went out into the desert. They took some bread and a skin full of water and then wandered off, not knowing where they were supposed to go. Before long, the bread ran out, and then the water ran out, too. The desert sun was beating down and they were getting weaker and weaker. Soon, Ishmael couldn't walk any further. Hagar laid him down gently under a little tree, where at least he had some shade. She went and sat behind a rock because she couldn't bear to see her son die.

Ask Hagar to sit down on one side of the hall and Ishmael to lie down on the other.

Then Hagar cried out to God and he sent an angel to her. The angel said, 'What's the matter, Hagar? Don't be frightened: God has heard the voice of the boy where he is. Come on, pick him up and hold his hand, because God will make him the father of a great nation. Come and look!' Then God's angel showed Hagar that in the shadow of some rocks there was a cool, deep spring. Hagar ran to Ishmael and carried him to the water: they drank and knew that they were going to be all right. God continued to watch over Ishmael and he grew up in the desert to become a strong young man.

Invite Ishmael to stand up and strike a 'strong man' pose.

Miles away, Isaac stayed with Abraham and Sarah and he grew up big and strong, too.

Invite Isaac to stand up and strike a 'strong man' pose.

When they were both grown-up, the two brothers had families of their own, and their descendants are still alive today.

Give all your volunteers a round of applause and ask them to sit down.

TWO BROTHERS – ISAAC AND ISHMAEL

The Point

God promised that Abraham's boys would become the fathers of great nations, and they did: Isaac grew up and became the father of the Jews and Ishmael became the father of Islam. These days, the news is full of stories about terrorism and war between different religions, but the story of Abraham and his sons is told by Christians, Jews and Muslims alike. It reminds us that we have lots in common.

The Prayer

Our prayers today will remind us that different religions have common ground. We will pray for peace in three different languages. Each of these words means 'Peace': can you say them after me?

Encourage everyone to repeat each word after you.

In Hebrew, it's 'Shalom'.
In Arabic, it's 'Salaam'.
In English, it's 'Peace'.

We'll repeat these three words, like this: 'Shalom, Salaam, Peace.'

Encourage everyone to repeat this line.

Now, in our prayer, I want you to repeat this line three times. Let us pray.

O God, in different languages our different nations pray for the same thing:
Shalom, Salaam, Peace,
Shalom, Salaam, Peace,
Shalom, Salaam, Peace.
Amen.

Song

'Let's join hands around the world'[8]

Plus

Suggestions for optional extras:

MUSIC   'We bring our prayers'[9]

---

8. Val Hawthorne, *30 Catchy New Assembly Songs*, Kevin Mayhew 2009
9. Alison Carver, *30 Catchy Assembly Songs*, Kevin Mayhew 2009.

The Big Fight
Jacob wrestles with an angel

The Plot

Jacob steals his older brother's birthright and his father's blessing, then runs away. His brother Esau arms himself for battle and pursues him. The night before the battle, Jacob meets a stranger who wrestles with him all night. He doesn't give up, and as the sun comes up the stranger blesses Jacob and gives him a new name: Israel.

(Genesis 32—33:4)

The Point

Faith isn't always easy: sometimes it can feel like a wrestling match with God, but God won't give up on us.

Story

I've got a story for you today. If you want to hear it, shout, 'What's the story?'

Encourage all to shout: **What's the story?**

This story is called 'The Big Fight' and it begins with two brothers called Jacob and Esau. Can you put your hand up if you've got a brother?

Invite responses.

Do you always get on well with your brother?

Invite responses.

Jacob and his brother Esau were twins, but they really didn't get on well at all. In fact, this story begins with Jacob, terrified that his brother is going to kill him. Can I have two volunteers to be Jacob and Esau?

Bring forward your two volunteers.

Here's Esau, the twin who was born first, on the warpath with 400 men by his side. Can you all be Esau's army? You need to wave your fists in the air, as if you're shaking your spears.

Encourage Esau and everyone in the assembly hall to wave their fists in a warlike manner.

And here's Jacob. He's sent his family on ahead before the battle, so now he's all on his own.

Encourage everyone to say: **Aaaaaah!**

But let's not feel too sorry for him. Do you know what he did? He was jealous of his older brother because he wanted Esau's *birthright* – the special rights that belong to the eldest son and make him the most important. So when Esau was really hungry one day, Jacob gave him some stew in exchange for his birthright. That made Jacob more important, but he still needed his father's blessing. His father was old and blind, so guess what? Jacob dressed up like Esau and tricked his father into giving him Esau's blessing! So Jacob managed to steal everything that belonged to his older brother. That's why Jacob ran away, and that's why Esau wants to kill him!

Now let's tell our story. We've got a very angry Esau and his army heading across the desert. They make camp for the night.

Encourage more warlike fist-waving, then ask Esau to sit down.

And we've got Jacob, all alone. It's dark and he's terrified, so he prays to God.

Jacob kneels down to pray.

He says, 'O God of my father and my grandfather, you told me you would look after me! I don't deserve your love and faithfulness, but I'm here now, and my brother's coming to get me. I'm scared – please save me from him! He'll kill me and my whole family. But you said you'd look after me, and give me as many descendants as there are grains of sand on the seashore.' It's true – God had promised he'd make Jacob the father of an enormous family that would spread all over the world.

Now Jacob is ready for the battle in the morning. But the fight comes sooner than he expects: a stranger grabs him! Can I have a volunteer to be this mysterious stranger?

Bring forward your volunteer and Jacob.

The stranger wrestles with Jacob until dawn. Let's freeze-frame this fight action.

Arrange your volunteers in a still fighting position – perhaps with arms locked on each other's shoulders, as in a rugby scrum. They need to hold this position.

Does anyone here do Judo or Taekwondo or any other martial art?

Invite responses.

How long do your classes last?

Invite responses.

WHAT'S THE STORY?

How would you feel if you had to practise your martial art *all night*?

Invite responses.

Well, that's how Jacob feels. But there is no winner, so he and the stranger keep on fighting. Then the stranger hits Jacob's hip and knocks it out of joint, and even though they've been fighting all night, Jacob says, 'I won't let go until you give me a blessing.'

The stranger asks, 'What's your name?'

'Jacob,' he answers.

The stranger tells him, 'From now on, your name will be Israel, because you've struggled with God and with people and won.'

Jacob says, 'Who are you?'

The stranger replies, 'Do you need to ask?' Then he blesses Jacob. At last, Jacob lets go and the fight is over.

Bring forward the stranger.

Who do you think the stranger is?

Invite suggestions, then ask the stranger to sit down, with a round of applause.

Let's see what Jacob thinks. Jacob struggles to his feet, because his hip hurts. He says, 'I've seen God face to face and survived!' Just then, Esau and his army arrive – but instead of fighting, the twin brothers hug each other.

Invite your Esau volunteer to stand and hug Jacob, then give them both a round of applause.

You lot with your spears aren't going to fight a battle after all.

The Point

The Bible describes the stranger who fought Jacob as a man and also an angel[10], but Jacob recognised him as God himself. He gave Jacob the special name of God's chosen people: Israel. The name may mean 'struggles with God' and it is still used to describe Jewish people and their homeland today. Jacob's story reminds us that faith isn't always easy. Sometimes we do bad things, or bad things happen to us, and then it can feel as if we are fighting with God. But like the stranger who held on to Jacob and blessed him, God never lets go – he will never give up on us.

---

10. Hosea 12:4

The Prayer

For our prayer today, we'll put our hands together – but not in the usual way. As we have been thinking about Jacob wrestling with God, I want you to clasp your own hands hard together as if you are in an arm-wrestling match.

Demonstrate and encourage everyone to do so.

As our hands wrestle each other, let's pray for everyone who is having a difficult time and anyone who is finding it hard to believe.

Pause.

God, hold on to us and never let us go.
Amen.

Song

'God is good'[11]

> ## Plus
>
> *Suggestions for optional extras:*
>
> **MUSIC**   'Don't be afraid'[12]

---

11. Barry Hart, *Sing the day through*, Kevin Mayhew 2009.
12. Val Hawthorne, *Sing the day through*, Kevin Mayhew 2009.

The Dreamer
Joseph's colourful life

The Plot

Joseph begins life as the favourite of twelve brothers and a dreamer of vivid dreams. His brothers plot to murder him, then sell him instead. He is taken to Egypt as a slave. Promotion follows – he becomes the boss of an Egyptian official's household – until he is wrongly accused and sent to prison. Behind bars, he interprets dreams. When he explains the dreams of Pharaoh himself, he becomes Pharaoh's right-hand man who oversees Egypt's food supplies. Record-breaking harvests are followed by famine and Joseph's starving brothers come to Egypt to buy food. Joseph tests them, then reveals himself as their long-lost brother. The whole family settles in Egypt.

(Genesis 37–50)

The Point

This is the story of how the Jews came to Egypt. It shows that in spite of his life's ups and downs, Joseph and his family were looked after by God.

Story

I've got a story for you today. If you want to hear it, shout, 'What's the story?'

Encourage all to shout: **What's the story?**

This story is called 'The Dreamer' and it is about a young man called Joseph. He had eleven brothers, but he was his dad's favourite. His dad's name was Jacob. Once, Jacob gave Joseph an expensive, multicoloured coat, just for him, as a special treat. His brothers didn't get anything. Was that fair?

Invite responses.

Joseph used to have strange dreams. One morning, he said, 'Guess what I dreamed last night!' His brothers groaned.

Encourage everyone to groan.

Joseph said, 'I dreamed that we were in the field, making sheaves of corn, and all your sheaves of corn bowed down to my sheaf!' The next morning, Joseph piped up again, 'Guess what I dreamed last night!' His brothers groaned again.

Encourage everyone to groan.

Joseph said, 'I dreamed that the sun, the moon and eleven stars were bowing down to me!' Let's try to picture these dreams. Can I have a volunteer to be Joseph?

Pick a volunteer right in the middle of the assembly hall and ask him/her to stand up.

Imagine that this is Joseph. In his dream, sheaves of corn and stars bowed down to him. If you'd like to be a tall, ripe sheaf of corn, can you stretch your arms up tall and wave your fingers, like this?

Demonstrate this action and encourage others to join in.

And if you'd like to be the stars, can you stretch up your arms and make star shapes with your hands, like this?

Demonstrate this action and encourage others to join in.

Now choose whether you'd like to be a sheaf of corn or some stars. Then turn to face Joseph and bow down to him!

Everyone chooses an action, then the whole hall bows to Joseph from a seated position.

Joseph, how does that feel?

Invite your volunteer to respond, then ask him/her to sit down.

If you were one of Joseph's brothers, hearing about those dreams, how would you feel?

Invite responses.

Well, Joseph's brothers were so jealous that they even thought about killing him. Instead, they grabbed his coat and dumped him in a pit in the desert, then sold him to some passing slave traders. Did he deserve that?

Invite responses.

The brothers went home and told their father that his favourite son was dead. Meanwhile, Joseph became a slave in Egypt, where he worked so hard that he became the boss of an important Egyptian soldier's household. Life was good – but then the soldier's wife told lies about Joseph and he was thrown into prison. Can we have another volunteer to be Joseph, please?

WHAT'S THE STORY?

Choose another child in the middle of the hall and ask him/her to stand up.

I need everyone around Joseph to hold up their arms like prison bars.

Encourage the rows immediately in front and behind your volunteer to do this.

So Joseph was in prison, but his jailer liked him and so did the other prisoners. Two of them had strange dreams and Joseph explained what they meant. The dreams came true, just as Joseph said, but he stayed in prison for two more years. He thought everyone had forgotten about him.

Ask Joseph to sit down. All those who made the prison bars lower their arms.

Egypt was ruled by the Pharaoh. One night he had some very strange dreams. Pharaoh dreamt that seven fat cows came out of the River Nile. Can you all make a big noise like happy, well-fed cows?

Encourage loud mooing.

After the seven fat cows, Pharaoh dreamt that seven skinny, ill-looking cows came out of the Nile. Can you all make a little noise like weak, hungry cows?

Encourage feeble mooing.

Guess what? The skinny cows ate the fat cows, but they still looked thin and ill! CANNIBAL COWS! Pharaoh was so scared, he woke up. When he dropped off to sleep again, he had another dream. This time it was about corn: seven fat, plump ears of corn came out of the Nile, followed by seven thin, weedy ears of corn. The same thing happened: the thin ones ate the fat ones but still looked just as skinny.

Pharaoh got up and yelled for all his magicians and wise men to tell him what these dreams meant, but none of them could. Then someone remembered a man in prison who knew all about dreams. Who was he?

Encourage everyone to shout: **Joseph!**

Pharaoh sent for Joseph, and Joseph told him the meaning of his dreams: Egypt would have seven years of bumper harvests, followed by seven years of famine. Everyone would starve unless they saved as much food as they could in the good years, to keep them alive during the famine. So Pharaoh put Joseph in charge of all Egypt's food and farming. There followed seven years of huge harvests, just as Joseph had said. Barns overflowed with grain and Joseph carefully stored all the spare food, so when the famine came, the people of Egypt still had enough to eat – all thanks to Joseph.

Encourage everyone to cheer.

Unfortunately, Joseph's family back home wasn't so well off. His father and brothers were starving. So they went to Egypt to beg for food. They were met by Pharaoh's right-hand man, Joseph: he knew them at once, but they didn't recognise their own brother, because he looked so grand and important! They bowed down to him. Can we have another volunteer to be Joseph?

Choose a volunteer in the middle of the hall and ask him/her to stand up.

Now, the rest of you are Joseph's brothers: can you bow down to him?

Encourage everyone to bow to Joseph, then ask your volunteer to sit down.

So you see, Joseph's dreams came true: his brothers bowed down to him, just like the stars and sheaves of corn in his dreams. Joseph remembered how his brothers had nearly killed him, then made him a slave. He tested them to see if their hearts were true. When he saw how sorry they were, he said, 'I am Joseph, your long-lost brother!' He opened his arms and hugged them all. He forgave them everything they had done to him, and shared his home, his food and his money with them. The whole family settled in Egypt with Joseph – even his dad, Jacob, who was a very old man. Joseph and his brothers had families of their own. They were the twelve tribes of Israel, and Joseph's story is the story of how Israel – or the Jewish nation – came to live in Egypt.

The Point

Joseph's life was what we might call 'colourful': it was full of dramatic events, high points and low points. Just think about all the different parts he played in his time: he began as a dreamer and a favourite. He nearly became a murder victim, but instead ended up a slave. Next he was a boss, then a prisoner and an interpreter of dreams. He became Pharaoh's right-hand man and then revealed himself as a long-lost brother. And yet God was watching over him all the time, and in the end Joseph's huge family, with its twelve tribes, grew into a great nation. They were God's chosen people. Joseph's story reminds us that God never gives up on us, no matter what ups and downs we face in our lives.

The Prayer

Our prayers today will be colourful, like Joseph's coat. Look around you at all the different colours you can see, and choose one that shows how you are feeling today. For example, if you are feeling happy, you might pick a bright colour like yellow or pink. If you are feeling sad, you might choose black or blue. If you are feeling cross, you might choose an angry red colour. Pick a colour and think about how you are feeling today. *(pause briefly)* Now let's pray.

Father God,
you know how we're feeling today.
Help us to remember that you never gave up on Joseph,
and you'll never give up on any of us,
whatever happens.
Amen.

WHAT'S THE STORY?

Song
'Don't be afraid'[13]

> **Plus**
>
> *Suggestions for optional extras:*
>
> **PROPS** Lots of paint colour sample charts to use as a prompt for the prayer.
>
> **MUSIC** 'He's got the whole world in his hand'

---

13. Val Hawthorne, *Sing the day through*, Kevin Mayhew 2009.

Blood, Bugs and Boils
The Ten Plagues of Egypt

The Plot

The Jews are suffering as slaves in Egypt and God decides to rescue them. He picks Moses to ask Pharaoh to let his people go. Pharaoh refuses again and again, so God strikes Egypt with ten terrible plagues. At last Pharaoh sends the Jews away and they are led by Moses to the wilderness and freedom.

(Exodus 3–12)

The Point

God is all-powerful.

Story

I've got a story for you today. If you want to hear it, shout, 'What's the story?'

Encourage all to shout: **What's the story?**

This story is called 'Blood, Bugs and Boils'. There are some really yucky, disgusting things in it – are you sure you want to hear it?

Invite responses.

Well, you've been warned. This story starts long, long ago with God's chosen people, the Jews. They were slaves in Egypt and they had to work hard all day. They had bruises on their backs, sores on their hands and blisters on their feet. God heard their cries for help and he decided to rescue them. He needed someone to lead his people, so he picked a man called Moses. Do you know how he got Moses' attention? Moses was herding sheep in the desert when *WOOOMPF!* A bush burst into flames, but didn't burn up. Moses stared at the strange fire, and God's voice said, 'Moses! Moses! Hey, you! I've got a job for you. Go and ask Pharaoh to let my people go.'

And Moses said, 'Who, me? No way.'

But God said, 'Yes, you. I'll tell you what to say and I'll show Pharaoh who's boss.'

So Moses went, terrified and trembling, to see Pharaoh in his royal palace. 'The Lord says, "Let my people go."'

Pharaoh roared, 'WHAT?! Your people are going nowhere – in fact, they've got to work twice as hard!'

WHAT'S THE STORY?

It was time for God to show Pharaoh who was *really* in charge. Are you ready for this? I'm going to need your help with sound effects. First of all, Moses went down to the River Nile, took his special wooden staff and touched the clear water. Now, I want a gloopy, bubbly sound effect like this: 'BLUB, BLUB, BLUB.'

Encourage everyone to make this sound.

That's the sound of water that has been turned to blood! The whole of the River Nile turned thick and red. Instead of running river water, there was gloopy gore! It went 'BLUB, BLUB, BLUB.'

Encourage everyone to make this sound.

It smelt like old plasters. Puddles turned into scabs, the fish all died and no one had any water to drink – even the water in the jugs had turned to blood. Moses said to Pharaoh, 'Now will you let my people go?'

Pharoah said, 'No!'

So next God sent a slippery swarm of frogs to invade Egypt. Can you make a noise like a million frogs?

Encourage lots of croaking.

There were frogs in the royal palace, frogs in the bedrooms, frogs in the beds! When people stepped outside their front doors, they slithered on frog slime; when they went to bake bread, there was frogspawn in the mixing bowls! Pharaoh said, 'Enough frogs! I'll let your people go!' So Moses called off the frogs, but Pharaoh changed his mind.

Then Moses sent a million midges to smother Egypt and everyone got bitten all day long. Can you imagine being surrounded by midges all the time? Use your hands as if you're waving the midges away from your faces.

Encourage everyone to wave imaginary midges away.

The midges drove the Egyptians mad. Moses said to Pharaoh, 'Now will you let my people go?'

Pharoah said, 'No!'

So then God made a billion buzzing flies swarm over Egypt. Can you make a noise like a billion flies?

Encourage lots of buzzing.

The flies filled the Egyptians' houses. You couldn't see for flies: if you sat down to eat, the flies fed on your dinner first, and if you opened your mouth to complain, flies flew in and got stuck in your teeth. Pharaoh said, 'Enough flies! I'll let your people go!' So Moses called off the flies, but Pharaoh changed his mind again.

So God sent a plague to infect all the Egyptians' animals. Donkeys died, cattle keeled over, camels kicked the bucket. Pharaoh still wouldn't free God's people, so God told Moses to send a plague on the Egyptians themselves. This one was horrible: everyone's skin was covered with big boils which were itchy, sore and smelly. The plague was like super-size chicken pox, with extra stinkiness. Ouch! Can you scratch as if you itch all over?

Encourage scratching.

Still Pharaoh would not let God's people go. So then God got to grips with the weather. He sent the heaviest hailstorms the world had ever seen, along with thunder and lightning. The hailstones were like cannon balls and they flattened every crop and tree. Out in the open, nothing and no one survived. Pharaoh said, 'Enough hail! I'll let your people go!' So Moses called off the storms, but Pharaoh changed his mind again.

New crops grew after the storms, but then God sent a swarm of locusts into Egypt. They turned the land black and ate every green thing in sight. Can you make a chomping noise like hungry locusts?

Encourage loud chomping noises.

There was nothing left to eat in the whole of Egypt. Pharaoh cried, 'Enough locusts! I'll let your people go!' So Moses called off the locusts, but Pharaoh changed his mind yet again.

Then God sent a deep darkness to cover Egypt. People couldn't tell whether it was day or night; for three days they couldn't see their hands in front of their faces. The country came to a standstill. Moses said to Pharaoh, 'Now will you let my people go?'

Pharoah said, 'NO! Now get away from me – I never want to see you again!'

Finally God sent the most terrible plague of all. He passed over Egypt and killed every firstborn animal and child. Even Pharaoh's eldest son died. The sound of crying came from every Egyptian house, but God did not touch the Jews. At last Pharaoh said to Moses, 'Get out! Go away and take all your people with you, before we all die!'

Moses gathered together every single one of God's people and led them all out into the wilderness, away from Egypt. They were free at last!

Encourage everyone to cheer.

The Point

This epic story of the ten plagues ends with a great event in the history of the Jewish people. When the Jews escaped from Egypt, they became a nation, led by Moses, and were free to worship God. For all of us, the story is a dramatic reminder that God is all-powerful. He hit Egypt with blood, bugs and boils and then rescued an entire nation. This shows that for God, nothing is impossible!

WHAT'S THE STORY?

The Prayer

For a really big, powerful God, sometimes we need a really big, powerful prayer. I'm going to teach you a prayer from the very end of the Bible, which the angels sing to God. It goes like this:

'Amen! Blessing and glory and wisdom
and thanksgiving and honour
and power and might
be to our God for ever and ever! Amen.'[14]

Ask everyone to repeat each line in turn after you, then say the first two lines together, then the second two, then all four lines.

Now we're ready to pray this really big prayer to our really big God. Let's say it in our biggest voices: LET US PRAY!

Everyone shouts:

AMEN! BLESSING AND GLORY AND WISDOM
AND THANKSGIVING AND HONOUR
AND POWER AND MIGHT
BE TO OUR GOD FOR EVER AND EVER! AMEN.

Song

'My God is so big'[15]

Plus

Suggestions for optional extras:

MUSIC   'When the raindrops fall'[16]

---

14. Revelation 7:12
15. Search the internet for words, melody and YouTube videos of accompanying actions.
16. Alison Carver, *30 Catchy New Assembly Songs*, Kevin Mayhew 2009.

The Great Escape
The Crossing of the Red Sea

The Plot

Moses leads God's people, the Israelites, out of Egypt and into the desert. The Egyptian army pursues them. By the shores of the Red Sea, the army closes in, so God gives Moses the power to divide the sea. The Israelites walk safely across on the sea bed, but the waters flood back and drown the Egyptians. God's people are free at last.

(Exodus 13:17–14:31)

The Point

God looks after his people.

Story

I've got a story for you today. If you want to hear it, shout, 'What's the story?'

Encourage all to shout: **What's the story?**

This story is called 'The Great Escape' and it's all about how the Jews finally escaped from slavery in Egypt. The story begins in the wilderness, where the whole nation of Israel followed Moses. Can you all stand up?

Encourage everyone to stand up.

Imagine that you are the Israelites. You're standing in the hot sun, wondering where you're going to go next. There are rocks, sand and scrubby grass stretching behind you as far as you can see. Ahead of you is the sea: tall reeds grow along the shore, but you can't see much further because the sun is glittering so fiercely on the water that it dazzles you. It reminds you how thirsty you are. I want each of you to imagine that you're standing here with your whole family and all your pets, and that you're carrying everything you can – as many clothes, precious toys and useful bits and bobs from home as you can hold. You're so hot and tired from walking through the desert, I think you need to sit down and rest. That's what God's people did – they made a camp by the sea.

Encourage everyone to sit down again.

WHAT'S THE STORY?

Meanwhile, back in Egypt, Pharaoh was furious. He'd just lost all his workers! Now that the slaves had escaped, who would finish building his great cities and his pyramid? He called for his chariot and summoned his army. His officers whipped their horses hard and over 600 chariots raced out into the wilderness, followed by soldiers who were armed to the teeth. All those hooves, wheels and feet kicked up a great cloud of sand, and when the Israelites saw the cloud, they knew that the Egyptians had come to hunt them down.

PANIC! There was an army behind them and a sea in front of them; night was falling and God's people were trapped! They screamed at Moses, 'Help! This is your fault! Why did you drag us out of Egypt? Now they're going to kill us all!
Moses said, 'Don't be afraid! God will rescue us!'

Then God told Moses to take his great wooden staff and stretch out his hand over the sea.

Stretch out your hand.

All night, God drove a fierce wind at the sea, until the waters divided. Can you move apart to make a path, like the waves did?

Encourage the children to move apart and clear a narrow path through the assembly hall.

Now can you stretch your hands up like the walls of water?

Encourage the children to do this, then walk slowly along the path as you continue with the story, returning to the front of the hall just before the Egyptians are drowned.

God made a miraculous path on the sea bed. On either side, there was a wall of water, held back by the wind. Very nervously, the Israelites followed Moses down onto the sea path. As they walked along, they looked deep into the blue walls of water. Shoals of silver fish flashed past, making the children jump. They could see jellyfish waving their tentacles hungrily at them. Crabs scuttled from under their feet and back into the coral. In the dim distance, huge creatures with big, blunt heads were swimming slowly through the reeds. High above, waves splashed and churned, as if they couldn't wait to crash down on top of the scurrying people who had never before set foot on the sea bed.

At last, the Israelites reached the other side. They turned to see the Egyptians, with their chariots and swords, struggling to make their way across the sand and rocks but getting closer with every moment. Then God told Moses to stretch out his hand over the sea again.

Stretch out your hand.

As the sun began to peep above the horizon, Moses stretched out his hand and the walls of water wobbled and collapsed with a great crashing and splashing of waves. The sea covered the whole of Pharaoh's army and every single soldier was drowned.

Encourage the children to lower their hands and move back to close the path.

As the day dawned, the Israelites realised that God had rescued them once and for all. There was no more doubt: everyone believed in God and everyone trusted Moses. They all joined in the biggest song of praise they had ever sung: it was a great big 'Hooray!' for their great God and their great escape.

After a count of three, all shout: **Hooray!**

The Point

For Jews and Christians, the story of the great escape – also known as the Exodus – is very important. It reminds them that God always looks after his people. Christians believe that we are all God's people, so whenever we face suffering or danger, whenever we're panicking or giving up hope, we can all take comfort from this story. Since God rescued his people and led them to freedom, he can help us, too.

The Prayer

We're used to putting our hands together for a prayer. I'd like you to put your hands together now, as we think about the Israelites in our story, trapped in front of the sea. Press your hands together tightly, and then bring them close to one eye. Try to peep through the little gap between your thumbs. You can't see anything but dark: neither could the Israelites, when they looked at the sea at night, with no way across – until God miraculously divided the waters and let them through. Move your hands slightly apart now so that you can see light between them: that's how it must have looked to the Israelites, walking between walls of water to freedom. We'll put our hands together now to pray.

Loving God,
we pray for everyone who feels stuck in a dark place.

Pause.

Now let's open our hands.

Everyone parts their hands.

Saving God,
open up a new path and show us the way out of the dark.
Amen.

WHAT'S THE STORY?

Song

'If I had a song I'd sing it'[17]

> **Plus**
>
> *Suggestions for optional extras:*
>
> **IT** There is a dramatic sequence showing the crossing of the Red Sea in the animated retelling of the Exodus, *The Prince of Egypt* (Dreamworks, 1999). You may like to show a short clip or a still image of the walls of water towering above the Israelites.
>
> **MUSIC** 'My God is a great big God'[18]

---

17. Val Hawthorne, *30 Catchy New Assembly Songs*, Kevin Mayhew 2009.
18. Search the internet for words, melody and YouTube videos of accompanying actions.

The Giant
David and Goliath

The Plot

It's the day of the big battle: Philistines v Israelites. The Philistine champion is a giant called Goliath. David – a shepherd-boy – takes him on, armed with nothing but a slingshot and five stones. The first stone knocks Goliath out with a blow between the eyes. David kills the giant with his own sword and cuts off his head. The Israelites win the day.

(1 Samuel 17:1-51)

The Point

However small you feel, don't be afraid.

Story

Place a chair or a table at the front of the hall.

I've got a story for you today. If you want to hear it, shout, 'What's the story?'

Encourage all to shout: **What's the story?**

Now, are you feeling brave?

Invite responses.

Are you feeling big and strong?

Invite responses.

I hope so, because this story is called 'The Giant'! The giant's name was Goliath and he was ENORMOUS. Let's try and imagine this giant: who is the tallest teacher in this school?

Invite responses, then ask the teacher to stand at the front and ask him how tall he is.

Now, to help us imagine Goliath, let's look at what the Bible tells us. First of all, how tall is he? The Bible says 'Six cubits and a span' which – depending on your cubit – could be anything from 6′ 9″ to 9′ 9″. That's nearly 3 metres tall! That's taller than *(teacher's name)*, so we need something for our volunteer giant to stand on.

WHAT'S THE STORY?

Invite the teacher to stand on a chair or a table.

Imagine a man who is *this* tall! But that's not all: we've got to imagine him ready for battle, because Goliath is his army's champion. The Bible gives us a list of what he is wearing: see if you can imagine *(teacher's name)* wearing all this.[19] First of all, he's wearing a bronze helmet. Then his whole body is protected with chainmail armour which weighs 50kg – that's as heavy as two sheepdogs! He has bronze armour on his legs like metal shin-pads. Slung across his back, he has a bronze javelin like a small tree-trunk. The spear-head alone weighs over 6kg! Finally, Goliath's shield is so big that it's one man's job to carry it for him.

So here is our giant, Goliath. He is the champion of the Philistines, and behind him stands an army which is waiting to do battle with God's people, the Israelites. Can you help set the scene? I'd like you to be the Philistine army. Having Goliath at the front makes you feel very brave, so you're roaring and shouting at your enemies.

Encourage warlike shouting from your Goliath volunteer and the children.

This is what happens next. Goliath strides up to Israel's soldiers and their king, Saul. He roars, 'Come on, then! Who's up for a fight? If anyone takes me on and beats me, my soldiers will become your slaves, but if I win, you will be ruled by us. I defy you all! Give me your best soldier, and let the battle begin!'

Well, would you volunteer? The men of Israel look at each other, terrified. Even the strongest man would be no match for Goliath. Then a boy's voice pipes up, 'I'll go!' It's David, a young shepherd-boy. Who would like to volunteer to be David?

Bring forward your smallest volunteer.

David is small but determined. The king looks him up and down and says, 'No way. He'll make mincemeat of you.' But David shows him his slingshot, which is a kind of catapult.

Show your volunteer how to mime shooting a stone from a sling, by whirling the sling around your head and then releasing one end.

'See this?' he says. 'This has killed lions and bears. I used to look after my father's sheep, and sometimes wild animals would steal the lambs. I chased them and shot a stone at them with this. One well-aimed stone will bring down the biggest beast. I've never missed – and I've never lost a single lamb. God saved me from lions and bears, and he will not let this Philistine hurt me.'

So the king agrees. He dresses David in the best armour, but it is so big and heavy that he can hardly walk. David throws it all off. Instead, he picks up his slingshot and five small, smooth stones. Then he walks towards Goliath.

The Philistine soldiers roar with laughter.

---

19. See 1 Samuel 17:4-7. For these calculations, I have assumed the weight of a shekel is 10g (archaeological finds suggest something around this figure).

Encourage everyone to laugh loudly.

'Is this a joke?' yells the giant. 'Come here, little boy, and I'll turn you into food for vultures!'

David yells back, 'You have weapons on your side, but I have God on mine! He will give me the power to kill you and my army will destroy yours, so that everyone will know that God is with us.' Goliath takes a step closer.

Ask your volunteer to mime putting a stone in the sling and then whirling it around his head.

David puts a stone in his sling and whirls it round his head, faster and faster until BAM! The stone hits Goliath right between the eyes and he topples like a tree that's just been hit with an axe.

Encourage your volunteer Goliath to step off the chair or table and sit down on it, slumped as if unconscious. Bring your volunteer David to stand triumphantly over him.

THUD! The giant lies unconscious at David's feet. Quick as a flash, David takes Goliath's sword, kills him and cuts off his head. The Philistines run away in terror, but the Israelite army – that's you, now – cheer for their hero, David the giant-killer!

Encourage everyone to cheer and applaud your volunteers.

The Point

David was a young boy and Goliath was a giant, but David won the battle because he trusted God to look after him. This story reminds us that however small and weak we feel, we needn't be afraid, because God can do amazing things.

The Prayer

For our prayers today, we're going to make ourselves as small as we can. Where you're sitting, can you curl yourself up into a tiny ball? That's how small David felt, compared to Goliath. Sometimes we can feel small, too, when there are big, scary, difficult things in our lives. Let's stay in that small shape as we pray.

God, who saved David from lions, bears and giants,
look after us when we feel small
make us strong when we feel weak
and teach us not to be afraid.
Amen.

WHAT'S THE STORY?

Song

'David was a young boy'[20]

> ### Plus
>
> *Suggestions for optional extras:*
>
> **IT** Search Google Images for a dramatic picture of David and Goliath.
>
> **PROPS** A home-made slingshot or a picture of one would be a useful visual aid.
>
> **MUSIC** 'Goliath was big and Goliath was strong'[21]

---

20. Alison Carver, *Sing the day through*, Kevin Mayhew 2009.
21. *Anglican Hymns Old & New*, Kevin Mayhew 2008.

'QUAKE! WIND! FIRE!
The prophet Elijah meets God in the desert

The Plot

Elijah has had enough of being God's prophet. No one is listening to him and now he's a wanted man, so he runs away and hides in the desert. However, God won't let his spokesman off the hook. He arrives with an earthquake, wind and fire, but his voice is in the silence that follows. He tells Elijah to go home and get on with the job.

(1 Kings 19:1-15)

The Point

Listen out for God.

Story

I've got a story for you today. If you want to hear it, shout, 'What's the story?'

Encourage all to shout: **What's the story?**

This story is more like a big film full of special effects. It's called ''QUAKE! WIND! FIRE!' Before we can tell this story together, I'm going to need your help. I need you to help me make the special effects. First of all, there is the sound of a whirlwind. Think of hurricanes, tornadoes and howling gales: can you whistle and whoosh like a whirlwind? When I want you to stop, I'll do this *(demonstrate a clear hand signal to indicate 'stop')*. Now, whirlwind sound effect – go!

Encourage all to make the sound of a whirlwind, then give the signal to stop.

Now, for the earthquake, we need a special effect you'll hear and feel. I want you to drum your feet on the floor to make a rumbling sound. If we do it right, you'll feel the floor shake! Watch out for the same signal to stop. Are you ready? Earthquake sound effect – go!

Encourage all to make the rumble of an earthquake, then give the signal to stop.

Finally, our story features a wildfire. For this, we'll need a visual special effect to show how the flames spread. Can you all wave your hands in the air like big flames?

Encourage all to stretch their arms up and wave their hands, then give the signal to stop.

WHAT'S THE STORY?

Now, let's start the waving flames on this side of the hall.

Indicate one side of the hall and encourage every pupil at the end of their row to wave their hands.

Then the person next to you will start making their flames, and the person next to them, and so on, until it looks as if the whole row is on fire.

Encourage the 'flames' to spread along the rows until everyone is creating the wildfire effect. Give the signal to stop.

Now you are my fully-trained special effects team. Can you remember what you've got to do? When I say WIND, what will you do?

Encourage all to make the sound of a whirlwind, then give the signal to stop.

When I say EARTHQUAKE, what will you do?

Encourage all to make the rumble of an earthquake, then give the signal to stop.

And when I say WILDFIRE, what will you do?

Starting with the pupils on the ends of their rows, encourage the 'flames' to spread along the rows until everyone is creating the wildfire effect. Give the signal to stop.

Now, let's tell our story. This is a story about a man called Elijah. God chose him to be his prophet, or spokesman: it was Elijah's job to tell the truth to powerful people, but this was very dangerous. He fought against wicked rulers, unfaithful people and false prophets. When the queen of Israel threatened to kill him, Elijah was afraid. He decided that he'd had enough and he ran off into the desert.

The desert was a horrible place to be. Elijah trudged up and down rocky paths while the sun watched him like a fierce, unblinking eye. He ate insects and spent his days looking for water. He had never been so thirsty. He couldn't see any point in carrying on, so he asked God to let him die. Elijah lay down and fell asleep, but God sent an angel to keep him alive: the angel brought fresh bread and water.

The angel kept bringing him food and water until he was strong enough to travel. Elijah went to a great mountain and found a cave to sleep in. God's voice came to him there and said, 'What are you doing here, Elijah?'

Elijah replied, 'I've worked as hard as I can for you, God. Now your people have turned their backs on you, given up their worship and killed your prophets. I'm the only one left, and I'm next.'

God said, 'Go and stand on the mountain. I am coming.' Then there was a howling and a whistling, strong enough to make the earth shiver: a powerful WIND whipped the air.

Encourage everyone to make the sound of a howling wind, then give the signal to stop.

But God was not in the wind.

Then there was a rumbling and a trembling, violent enough to crack open the cave: a mighty EARTHQUAKE shook the mountain.

Encourage everyone to stamp their feet, then give the signal to stop.

But God was not in the earthquake.

Then there was a crackling and a roaring of flames that were hot enough to cook the rocks: a fierce WILDFIRE ripped around the mountain.

Encourage everyone to wave their arms in the air like flames, spreading from one side of the hall to the other, then give the signal to stop.

But God was not in the fire.

After the fire, there was a sound of sheer silence.

Put your finger to your lips and pause for a moment of silence, then speak quietly, in a stage whisper.

In the silence, there was a still, small voice. God said, 'What are you doing here, Elijah?'

Elijah sighed and said, 'I've worked as hard as I can for you, God. Now your people have turned their backs on you, given up their worship and killed your prophets. I'm the only one left, and I'm next.'

God said, 'Go. It's time to go back. There's work to do.' Elijah did as he was told.

Let's have a round of applause for our special effects team!

Encourage applause.

The Point

When Elijah was scared and alone in the desert, he talked to God. God answered in a surprising way: Elijah looked for him in the mighty wind, and the terrifying earthquake, and the fierce fire, but God was in the silence. Whenever we need help, we can talk to God, too. Like Elijah, we need to listen hard for his answer, because it might not come in the way we expect.

The Prayer

We are going to say a prayer together now. First of all, let's think about anyone we know who needs God's help.

Pause.

Let's think about the help we need, too.

Pause.

Our prayers today are going to be one big noisy cry for help. Think about who you are praying for and when I say, 'Let us pray,' we'll all take a deep breath and pray with one word: 'HELP!' You can shout it as loud as you like, or say it quietly. Now we pray for everyone who needs God's help. Let us pray.

(All together): **HELP!**

Pause.

Now, like Elijah in our story, we'll wait in the sheer silence after the noise and listen.

Put your finger to your lips and pause for a short time.

Amen.

Song

'Somebody needs my prayer today'[22]

Plus

Suggestions for optional extras:

IT — Display still pictures or footage of tornadoes, earthquakes and wildfire.

PROPS — Use a large pedestal fan to contribute to the wind effect. Provide some strips of flame-coloured fabric or crêpe paper and give them to volunteers to wave (standing at the front) for the fire effect.

MUSIC — 'Prayer's like talking on a mobile phone'[23]

---

22. Val Hawthorne, *Sing the day through*, Kevin Mayhew 2009.
23. Alison Carver, *Sing the day through*, Kevin Mayhew 2009.

Staying Alive
God saves three men from the fiery furnace

The Plot

The king of Babylon, Nebuchadnezzar, orders his people to worship a golden statue; any law-breakers will be thrown into a fiery furnace. Three young Israelites at the king's court, Shadrach, Meshach and Abednego, refuse to worship anyone but God. The king throws them into the fiery furnace but an angel protects them from the fire and they emerge unharmed.

(Daniel 3)

The Point

Trust in God.

Story

I've got a story for you today. If you want to hear it, shout, 'What's the story?'

Encourage all to shout: **What's the story?**

This story begins in a very hot place. Close your eyes, because I want you to imagine it: it's a place that the Bible calls 'the burning fiery furnace'. Imagine the enormous fire on Bonfire Night, burning inside a big pit. Over the pit is a brick dome that's big enough for several people to stand up in – but no one's in there at the moment, because the fire is roaring and it's so hot, it can melt metal. You could bend a sword like a piece of toffee. This is the burning fiery furnace, and if you stand too close to it, your eyebrows start to smoke. If you get any closer than that, your skin starts to sizzle like bacon. That's how hot it is. Now open your eyes. This story is about three men who were thrown into the burning fiery furnace – but it's called 'Staying Alive'! Let's find out what happened.

First of all, I need your help. Whenever I say 'BURNING FIERY FURNACE', can you make a roaring, whooshing noise like fierce flames? It should sound a bit like a rocket blasting off.

Demonstrate and encourage everyone else to join in.

That sound will remind us of the roaring flames in the BURNING FIERY FURNACE.

Everyone roars and whooshes like flames.

WHAT'S THE STORY?

Now it's time to meet the characters in our story. First of all, there is a cruel and bad-tempered king of Babylon called Nebuchadnezzar. This is how cruel and bad-tempered he is: he once had a bad dream and asked his wise men to explain it to him – but he wouldn't tell them what the dream was! He said they had to read his mind or he'd chop their heads off! This is the king in today's story, so whenever I say 'KING NEBUCHADNEZZAR', can you make a really cross face?

Encourage people to pull cross faces.

No, much crosser than that – you need to look so angry that you'd frighten people!

Encourage further face-pulling.

And relax. So remember, that's the face I want you to pull when I say 'KING NEBUCHADNEZZAR'.

Everyone pulls a cross face.

And finally, the three heroes of our story are Shadrach, Meshach and Abednego. They are three young Israelites who are working as wise men for the king. I'd like you to cheer whenever I say those three names: SHADRACH, MESHACH AND ABEDNEGO.

Everyone cheers.

This story began when KING NEBUCHADNEZZAR *(face-pulling)* built a giant, ugly statue out of pure gold. It was the biggest bit of bling that Babylon had ever seen. KING NEBUCHADNEZZAR *(face-pulling)* called all his people together to admire his statue and then he made a new law: 'When the music plays, that's the signal to fall down and worship my golden statue. Anyone who doesn't join in will be thrown into the BURNING FIERY FURNACE!' *(whooshing sound)*.

Well, when the music played, everyone fell down and worshipped the golden statue, apart from three young Israelites: SHADRACH, MESHACH AND ABEDNEGO *(cheering)*. KING NEBUCHADNEZZAR *(face-pulling)* was furious! He shouted, 'You'd better worship my statue or I'll throw you into the BURNING FIERY FURNACE *(whooshing sound)*. Who's going to save you then?'

SHADRACH, MESHACH AND ABEDNEGO *(cheering)* replied, 'We only worship God. If he'll save us from the BURNING FIERY FURNACE *(whooshing sound)*, then let him save us, but we're not going to worship your golden statue. No way.'

Then KING NEBUCHADNEZZAR *(face-pulling)* was so angry that his face twisted and turned purple! He ordered his men to take more fuel – not twice as much, and not three times as much, but seven times as much fuel as usual – and stoke up the BURNING FIERY FURNACE *(whooshing sound)* until it was white-hot. Then he ordered his strongest guards to throw in SHADRACH, MESHACH AND ABEDNEGO *(cheering)*. The heat was so fierce that the guards fell down dead, as into the heart of the fire tumbled SHADRACH, MESHACH AND ABEDNEGO *(cheering)*.

The king and his court looked through the door and watched what happened next. It was hard to see anything at all in the brightness and the heat, but then KING NEBUCHADNEZZAR *(face-pulling)* shouted, 'I thought there were three of them! Why can I see four men walking about in there? They're not hurt at all, and the fourth looks like some kind of angel! Oy, you three! Get out here right now!'

Then out of the BURNING FIERY FURNACE *(whooshing sound)* walked SHADRACH, MESHACH AND ABEDNEGO *(cheering)*. Not a hair on their head was singed, their skin was untouched and their clothes weren't sooty. They didn't even smell of smoke. Incredible! For once, KING NEBUCHADNEZZAR *(face-pulling)* didn't look cross – he looked amazed. He said, 'Bless the God who rescued these men! They disobeyed me and risked their lives rather than worship anyone else, and now look! He sent an angel to save them from the fire!' People looked at their king's astonished face and wondered whether he was going to be a different man from now on. Then he said, 'Right, I'm making a new law! If anyone says anything bad about the great God of SHADRACH, MESHACH AND ABEDNEGO *(cheering)* I'll tear their legs off and burn their house down!' He was the same KING NEBUCHADNEZZAR *(face-pulling)* after all.

The Point

The heroes of today's story completely trusted in God, and their amazing rescue showed that God rewarded their trust. We may not face fiery furnaces or cross, cruel kings – thank goodness – but we can always trust in God when things get tough.

The Prayer

When the heroes of our story looked into the burning fiery furnace, they must have covered their faces with their hands, like this.
Briefly cover your face with your hands.

This is something we all do from time to time, if we're feeling very scared or sad. For our prayers today, let's cover our faces with our hands and pray.

Wonderful God,
when we are sad or scared, help us to trust in you.
When we are lost or lonely, help us to trust in you.
Come to us and say, 'Don't be afraid.'
Amen.

Song

'This is your song'[24]

---
24. Barry Hart, *Sing the day through*, Kevin Mayhew 2009.

> **Plus**
>
> *Suggestions for optional extras:*
>
> **IT** Show images of blast furnaces.
>
> **MUSIC** 'Do you know?'[25]

---

25. Becky & Andy Silver, *Sing the day through*, Kevin Mayhew 2009.

Teeth and Claws
Daniel in the lions' den

The Plot

Daniel works hard for King Darius and wins promotion. Jealous court officials plot to get rid of him: they persuade King Darius to make an unbreakable law against praying to anyone other than the king. Daniel ignores this and prays faithfully to God, so the king reluctantly throws him into the lions' den. God sends an angel to protect Daniel and he escapes unharmed. King Darius throws the jealous officials to the lions instead and decrees that all his subjects must worship Daniel's God.

(Daniel 6)

The Point

Be brave, because God is looking after you.

Story

I've got a story for you today. If you want to hear it, shout, 'What's the story?'

Encourage all to shout: **What's the story?**

This story begins with a stony pit. I want you to imagine it, so close your eyes. This stony pit is dark and smelly: in fact, it's more than just a pit – it's a den. It smells like a cat's litter tray that hasn't been cleaned out for weeks! It also smells of rotten meat, because on the floor there are some big, chewed bones. One looks like an animal's leg. The others might be human arms . . . Now, picture what I've told you about this den – imagine the smell and the bones on the floor. Now open your eyes. If I tell you that the title of this story is 'Teeth and Claws', can you guess what kind of animals live in this den?

Invite suggestions.

In this dark, smelly, stony, bony den there lived a family of hungry lions. *(point to a small child)* The baby lions would eat you for breakfast. *(point to a bigger child)* The mummy lion would eat you for lunch. *(point to a senior teacher)* And the daddy lion would eat every bit of you for supper! But the lions' den belonged to a king, and the lions only ate when the king wanted to get rid of someone who had been bad. Then he fed them to the lions! It's what he used instead of a Naughty Step.

WHAT'S THE STORY?

The king had lots of important people who gave him advice, but the best of them all was Daniel. Daniel was good and kind and the people trusted him, so the king decided to give him the top job. This made the other advisers very jealous of Daniel. They complained, 'It's not fair! What makes *him* so special?' So they plotted to get Daniel into trouble. Big trouble. Trouble with teeth and claws.

The advisers made the king sign a new law: 'When you say your prayers, pray to the king. If you pray to God or anyone else, you'll be fed to the lions. By order of King Darius.' But Daniel prayed faithfully to God, and so the advisers told the king that Daniel must be thrown to the lions. King Darius really liked Daniel, but even the king wasn't allowed to break his own law, so he sadly agreed.

The lions got ready for their dinner. Guards threw Daniel into the den and sealed the stone over the entrance. He looked at the bones on the floor, he heard the lions' tummies rumbling and he was terrified; but he was not alone. God sent Daniel an angel – an angel who was more powerful than any lion. The angel stood firmly between Daniel and the lions, and the lions knew – as animals do – that he was the boss. They knew they wouldn't be getting any dinner tonight, so they retreated to the dark corners of the den and settled grumpily down to sleep. Daniel rested, too, but the angel stood guard all night.

In the morning, the king was amazed and delighted to find that Daniel was still alive. He rescued Daniel from the den and instead he threw in the advisers who had tricked him. The angel looked at the lions as he left and nodded his head, as if he were giving them permission. The hungry lions pounced and that was the end of the men who had tried to get rid of Daniel. Then King Darius made a new law: 'Daniel's God is the real, living God who works wonders in the world. He saved Daniel from the lions: now all my people must worship him. By order of King Darius.'

The Point

It's hard to imagine being as frightened as Daniel was, trapped in the den with a family of hungry lions, but God didn't leave him on his own. We all have times when we're frightened, when we have to face up to things that scare us. Daniel's story can help us to be brave, because it reminds us that God is always looking after us. He may not send us an angel, but he will always help us.

The Prayer

God sent an angel to help Daniel in the lion's den. Can you use your hands to make the shape of an angel?

Demonstrate as you describe the following action.

Put both your hands up, palms forward, as if you're saying 'Stop!' Then link your thumbs together to make the body and spread out your fingers to make a great pair of wings, like this. I wonder whether the lions in our story were scared of those enormous wings? This was the angel God sent to help Daniel. When you need God's help, use your hands to help you remember the angel – then put your hands together like this and pray.

Put your hands together and encourage everyone to do the same.

Living God,

help us when we need you,

be strong for us when we're trying to be brave.

Remind us that nothing is more powerful than your love.

Amen.

Song

'Who is who?'[26]

> ## Plus
>
> *Suggestions for optional extras:*
>
> IT   A big picture or sound effect of a roaring lion.
>
> MUSIC   'Be bold, be strong'[27]

---

26. Val Hawthorne, *30 Catchy New Assembly Songs*, Kevin Mayhew 2009. This is a Bible who's who, and a useful song to sing at the end of this collection of Old Testament stories.
27. *Anglican Hymns Old & New*, Kevin Mayhew 2008.

Eaten Alive!
Jonah and the Big Fish

The Plot

God picks Jonah to go and give the people of Nineveh a warning: 'Watch out – God knows how badly you've been behaving.' Jonah doesn't want to help the Ninevites, who are Israel's enemies, so he runs away on board a ship heading in the opposite direction. God stirs up a great storm and the sailors decide it's Jonah's fault, so they throw him overboard. God sends a big fish to swallow Jonah whole. In the fish's belly, Jonah realises that he should have followed God's orders, and after three days the fish spits him out on dry land. Jonah heads to Nineveh and tells the people to repent, which they all do, so God forgives the city. Jonah sulks because God has shared his love and mercy with Israel's enemies. *(Jonah 1–4)*

The Point

Neither Jonah's reluctance, nor Nineveh's wrongdoing, nor its enmity towards Israel can stop God caring about the people of the city. Nothing gets in the way of God's love.

Story

I've got a story for you today. If you want to hear it, shout, 'What's the story?'

Encourage all to shout: **What's the story?**

This story is called 'Eaten Alive!' and it's about a man called Jonah. Can I have a volunteer to be Jonah?

Invite responses.

Jonah spent a lot of time looking grumpy and cross, so can I see your best grumpy faces?

Invite responses, and bring forward the volunteer with the grumpiest expression.

Now, here's Jonah. From the moment God picked him to do a special job, Jonah went into a sulk. You see, God noticed that the people who lived in a city called Nineveh were behaving very badly. They were stealing, lying, hurting each other and generally being very naughty indeed. God wanted Jonah to give them a warning: 'Watch out – God knows what you're up to!' But Jonah sulked.

EATEN ALIVE! – JONAH AND THE BIG FISH

Encourage Jonah to sulk.

He thought, 'Why should I help that lot in Nineveh? They're my people's enemies! If their badness means the end of them, that's fine by me!'

God said to Jonah, 'Go to Nineveh and give them my warning!'

Jonah replied, 'NO! You can't make me!'

God thought, 'We'll see about that.' Then Jonah ran away, as far away from God and Nineveh as he could get.

Encourage Jonah to run away by doing a lap of the assembly hall.

Jonah found sailors getting their ship ready to sail a very long way away. Can I have four volunteers to be sailors, please?

Bring forward your volunteers and stand them in rowing pairs with mimed oars. Jonah stands at one end of the boat and they mime rowing.

Jonah climbed aboard, reckoning that a long sea voyage was just the thing to get him away from God and Nineveh. But God had other ideas: he sent a huge storm to wreck the ship. I need all of you to make massive waves: can we send a Mexican wave down each row, so that this assembly hall looks like a stormy sea?

Start the Mexican waves off in each row of children and encourage them to keep the waves going as the story continues.

The sailors rowed hard against the waves.

Encourage your sailors to row harder.

Then the sailors looked at each other and said, 'Whose fault is this storm?' They pointed at Jonah and Jonah said, 'You're right! I'm trying to run away from God! Throw me overboard and the waves will calm down!' So the sailors threw Jonah into the sea, and immediately the waves stopped, the wind dropped and the sea was calm.

Ask Jonah to jump away from the sailors, tell the Mexican waves to stop and ask your sailors to stop rowing.

But God didn't want Jonah to drown, so he sent an enormous fish to swallow him whole. *(to the sailors)* Can you make a big fish's belly between you?

The sailors in pairs face each other and raise their arms together, as if making a triumphal arch after a wedding. This is the fish's rib cage: invite Jonah to stand or sit inside.

WHAT'S THE STORY?

Jonah was eaten alive! He sat inside the fish's belly for three days and three nights. At first, he sulked.

Encourage Jonah to sulk.

Then he had a long hard think about what he'd done, and he realised that it was no good trying to run away from God. He knew that God had caused the storm, but he'd also sent the fish to save him from drowning. Jonah promised God that he would go to Nineveh. At that, God told the fish to spit Jonah out, so the fish swam to dry land and spewed Jonah out on the beach. Can we have a big noise as the fish throws up Jonah?

Encourage everyone to shout: **Bleeeuurgh!** *Your sailor/fish belly volunteers sit down and Jonah comes forward.*

Jonah went straight to Nineveh and said to his enemies, 'Watch out – God knows what you're up to! If you don't say sorry and stop doing wrong, it'll be the end of you!' Now, I'd like all of you to be the people of Nineveh. You've heard God's message from Jonah and every single one of you is sorry. From the king to the cook's smallest slave, all of you want to change your ways. So after a count of three, I'd like all you people of Nineveh to look up to heaven and shout, 'SORRY!'

Count to three and all shout: **SORRY!**

God heard the people, loved them and forgave them all. He decided that none of them would be punished. God was very pleased, but Jonah was furious that his people's enemies had been forgiven! He went off in a huff.

Encourage Jonah to sulk.

He shouted at God, 'I knew this would happen! You are a loving and merciful God, and now you've forgiven that lot in Nineveh! That's why I never wanted to come here in the first place.'

God replied, 'There are thousands of people in this great city, and they didn't know what was what. Why shouldn't I care about them?' Jonah knew God was right, and that made him sulk all the more. There's no pleasing some people!

Encourage Jonah to turn his back in a huff, then applaud him and all your volunteers.

The Point

There were lots of reasons for God to give up on the people of Nineveh. First, they were the Jews' enemies. Second, they were behaving very badly. Third, Jonah didn't want to help God at all – he sulked, refused and tried to run as far away as possible. But God got his own way in the end, and the people of Nineveh were saved. This story reminds us that nothing can get in the way of God's love. He loves each of us, too, no matter who we are or what we've done.

The Prayer

For our prayers today, we will remember that nothing can get in the way of God's love. To help us, we'll use our hands to make a heart shape, like this. Can you put your thumbs together to form the bottom point and curl your fingers in to make the shape of a heart?

Demonstrate this and encourage everyone else to do the same.

Let's look at this heart shape and think about God's love as we pray.

God, your love is the strongest thing there is.
Help us to remember that nothing
can get in the way of your love for us.
Amen.

Song

'I could climb the Eiffel Tower'[28]

Plus

Suggestions for optional extras:

IT Show a picture of a sperm whale.

MUSIC 'Be my light when darkness is falling'[29]

---

28. Alison Carver, *30 Catchy New Assembly Songs*, Kevin Mayhew 2009.
29. Alison Carver, *30 Catchy New Assembly Songs*, Kevin Mayhew 2009.

Locusts and Honey
The story of John the Baptist and Advent

The Plot

John is living rough in the wilderness, eating wild food and wearing animal skins. God gives him an urgent message to deliver, because Jesus is coming: 'Get ready for the Lord!' John isn't shy about telling people – be they poor or powerful – that they've done wrong and need to repent. He baptises them in the River Jordan and becomes known as John the Baptist. He's a teller of inconvenient truths who ends up being executed by King Herod. *(Matthew 3:1-12; Luke 3:1-20; John 1:19-28; Mark 6:17-29)*

The Point

John wanted people to get ready for Jesus by saying sorry for what they'd done wrong. During Advent we can get ready to celebrate Jesus' birth by saying sorry, too.

Story

Before we hear our story today, I want to set the scene. Imagine that you're in a desert. It's a wilderness of rocks, sand and stones. There are one or two tiny streams here and there, hidden at the bottom of rocky valleys, and occasionally you might find a skinny little tree. All you can hear is the wind and the occasional scuttling of tiny desert creatures. There's nobody else around. It's not a place to get lost in, this wilderness: if people have to travel through it, they ride on camels and get to the next water hole as quickly as they can. Imagine that you're in this wilderness. What are you going to eat?

Invite suggestions.

What are you going to wear to protect you from the heat of the day and the cold at night?

Invite suggestions.

This story is about a man called John who was living rough in the wilderness. The Bible says that he wore camel skins to protect him from the sun and the cold. Now, these camel skins weren't like a posh fur coat. John had found a dead camel in the desert and cut off its skin! He dried it in the sun, but it was still crusty with camel blood and it smelled like rotten meat. In fact, wherever John went, a cloud of flies followed him and desert lions licked their lips.

LOCUSTS AND HONEY – THE STORY OF JOHN THE BAPTIST AND ADVENT

John was always hungry. We've heard some suggestions of desert food; the Bible tells us that John ate wild honey – and locusts! Now, people disagree about what this word means. Some think that John ate beans from the carob tree, which are also known as locust beans. They taste sweet, a bit like chocolate. Other people think that John actually ate the insects that look like big grasshoppers, which are eaten as tasty treats in some parts of the world. What do you think? Put your hand up if you think John ate some chocolatey beans to stay alive in the desert.

Invite responses.

And put your hand up if you think John ate locusts, with their crunchy heads and bristly legs.

Invite responses and assess which option has the more votes.

OK – *the beans/the insects* win! Now we're ready to tell this story. If you want to hear it, shout, 'What's the story?'

Encourage all to shout: **What's the story?**

This story is called 'Locusts and Honey'. It happened about thirty years after Jesus was born. Jesus was ready to do God's work among the people of Galilee, so God had an important message to deliver to them: 'Get ready! The Lord is coming!' God wondered who could deliver his message for him. The Roman Emperor? Maybe not. Pilate, the Roman Governor? Hmm. Herod, the ruler of Galilee? No, God chose none of these important men in their grand palaces. He picked an ordinary man called John who was wandering alone in the wilderness, wearing half a dead camel and eating *chocolatey beans/flying insects.*

John took God's message to the people: 'Get ready! The Lord is coming!'

The people replied, 'What do you mean?'

So John explained. 'Do the right thing! Say sorry for what you've done wrong and do good!' He gave them some examples: to the ordinary people, he said, 'Share: food, clothes, whatever you can.' To the greedy tax-collectors he said, 'Be fair: don't take more money than you should.' To the tough Roman soldiers he said, 'Spare us your threats: don't bully us for money.' He even said to King Herod, 'Don't you care? Your marriage is against the law.'

Some important priests came from Jerusalem and said to John, 'So are you God's Chosen One?'

'Not me,' replied John. Then he said to everyone, 'Beware: God is sending someone who is far more important than me. I'm not fit to lick the soles of his boots! He will sort you all out, make no mistake – good people on one side and bad people on the other. Which side are you on?'

John had a lot of fans and he baptised thousands of people in the River Jordan. He also had a lot of enemies. Herod threw him in prison, but no one hated him more than Herod's wife, because John had said her marriage was wrong. She decided he'd have to go – and her plan involved a big dinner tray.

WHAT'S THE STORY?

Mime or hold up a big tray.

Can you guess what she wanted to put on this dinner tray? I'll give you a clue – it wasn't John's locusts. It was something even more disgusting. Are you sure you want to know what it was?

Invite responses.

You'll find out what the queen put on this tray at the end of the story . . .

It was the king's birthday party and all his guests were there in their best party clothes. Deep down in the dungeon under the palace, John the Baptist could hear the music. Herod's beautiful step-daughter danced for the company, and Herod was so delighted by her dancing that he made her a promise: she could have anything she wanted. The girl didn't know what to say, so she asked the queen's advice. The queen whispered to her and she whispered to the king. The king whispered to his guards and they left the room. A short time later they came back from the dungeon with the princess' present on a dinner tray: it was John the Baptist's head!

The Point

John the Baptist wanted people to get ready for Jesus by saying sorry for what they'd done wrong. Christians tell his story during Advent, as they prepare to celebrate Jesus' birth at Christmas. Advent is a time for getting ready by saying sorry to God, and it's important for us all to say sorry for whatever we've done wrong.

The Prayer

Our prayers today will give us a chance to say sorry to God for whatever we have done wrong. As you think about what that might be, I'd like you to hold your hand tight like a fist. Imagine that inside your fist is whatever you're feeling sorry for: perhaps you've been unkind to someone, broken something or told a lie. You might be too sorry to tell anyone else, but you can tell God. Now we'll have a moment of quiet as you think of whatever it is in your fist and say sorry to God in your heart. Then open your hand and let it go. Let's pray together.

Demonstrate this gesture then encourage everyone to clench their fists, pause for a moment as they say sorry, then open their hands.

Now we'll say these words: 'May God forgive us. Amen.' All together:

Encourage everyone to join in.

May God forgive us.
Amen.

Song

'There's a word'[30]

> **Plus**
>
> *Suggestions for optional extras:*
>
> **IT** Show a picture of the Judean desert.
>
> **PROPS** A big dinner tray or tea tray.
>
> **MUSIC** 'Peter asked Jesus'[31]

---

30. Val Hawthorne, *Sing the day through*, Kevin Mayhew 2009.
31. Barry Hart, *30 Catchy New Assembly Songs*, Kevin Mayhew 2009.

The New Baby
The Christmas story

The Plot
God sends an angel to Mary with some big news: she will have a special baby called Jesus and he will be God's Son. Mary marries Joseph and together they travel to Bethlehem. They find temporary accommodation in a stable and there Jesus is born. Angels give the news to some local shepherds, who come and worship Jesus. Wise men from the east follow the new star that is shining over the stable; they bring gifts for the Son of God. *(Matthew 1:18–2:12; Luke 1:26–2:20; John 1:1-18, 3:16)*

The Point
Jesus' birth is good news for the whole world, because it shows that God loves us so much, he gave us his only Son.

Story

I've got a story for you today. If you want to hear it, shout, 'What's the story?'

Encourage all to shout: **What's the story?**

This story is called 'The New Baby' and it's a story we all know very well: the Christmas story. Can you put your hand up if you've ever acted in a Nativity play?

Invite responses.

Nativity plays are great fun: everyone gets a chance to dress up and have their starring moment on stage. Today we are going to tell the Christmas story in a new way. We haven't got a manger or a doll wrapped in blankets; we haven't got any head-cloths for the shepherds to wear; we haven't even got any tinsel haloes for the angels. But we have got all of you. Do you think you can help me tell the Christmas story using nothing but your hands?

Invite responses.

Put your hands up in the air!

Encourage everyone to do so.

THE NEW BABY – THE CHRISTMAS STORY

What a lot of hands! They are just what we need. We are going to tell the Christmas story with some sign language – this is a special language used by people who can't hear. I'm going to teach you the signs for the most important words in the Christmas story. There are seven of them, so are you concentrating? Here we go.

Demonstrate each sign, explaining what it shows if necessary, and encourage everyone to have a go.[32]

This is the sign for GOD. *(Index finger points outwards then flicks up.)*

This is the sign for BABY. *(Mime rocking a baby in your arms.)*

This is the sign for JESUS. *(Middle finger of right hand touches centre of left palm, then vice versa – pointing at the places where the nails went in.)*

This is the sign for ANGEL. *(Hands held up with open palms, crossing at the wrist; hands flap like wings.)*

This is the sign for SHEPHERD. *(With a closed fist, mime the shape of a shepherd's crook, starting by moving up the shaft and then around the curly crook.)*

This is the sign for STAR. *(Holding your hands above your head, join index fingers and thumbs together to make a diamond shape.)*

This is the sign for KING. *(Clawed hand touches the top of your head and then moves off, miming the removal of a crown.)*

Now we're ready to tell the story, and I want you all to join in with the right sign every time you hear one of these important words.

Once upon a time, in the beginning, there was GOD. He loved the world he'd made and he wanted to show us his love, so he decided to give us his Son. God sent an ANGEL to earth with a message for a woman called Mary. The message was, 'Mary, you're going to have a BABY. He will be a KING and the Son of GOD. His name will be JESUS.'

Mary was very shocked. Joseph, the man she was going to marry, was very upset. But the ANGEL explained to him that this was going to be a very special BABY, so Joseph married Mary and together they travelled to Bethlehem, his home town.

Mary and Joseph couldn't find anywhere to stay in Bethlehem. Then Mary said, 'Joseph, the BABY is coming!' They found some shelter in a stable. On the straw, surrounded by animals, JESUS was born.

The ANGEL was still at work. He went to the hills near Bethlehem where there were lots of SHEPHERDS. The angel shouted, 'Good news! Your Saviour has just been born! He's in Bethlehem, in a manger!' All of a sudden, the skies were filled with ANGELS singing songs of praise. Can you all make the sign high above your heads, so that the air is full of ANGELS?

---

32. I have referred to www.britishsignlanguage.com for most of these signs: there are helpful pictures demonstrating each one. See also an illuminating YouTube video by DeafClergy.org.uk, showing a signed performance of 'While Shepherds Watched Their Flocks By Night.'

WHAT'S THE STORY?

Encourage everyone to make the sign for 'angel' above their head.

So the SHEPHERDS rushed to the stable. They bowed down and worshipped the BABY.

Outside, high in the sky, a bright new STAR was shining. Wise men far away knew it meant that a KING had been born. They travelled across the desert to Bethlehem, following the STAR. When they reached the stable, they gave rich gifts to the BABY. Then they bowed down before JESUS, the Son of GOD.

Invite everyone to use their hands one more time and give themselves a round of applause.

The Point

No matter how well we know it, the Christmas story is always worth retelling, because it reminds us that God loves us so much, he gave us his only Son. At Christmas, we celebrate Jesus' birth because it is good news for everyone!

The Prayer

For our prayer today, we'll use the signs we learnt for our story: *(encourage everyone to make the signs as you say the words)* GOD, ANGEL, STAR, SHEPHERD, BABY, JESUS, KING. Listen out for these words in our prayer. Let us pray.

GOD, our Father,
thank you for Christmas.
Thank you for the ANGEL and the STAR,
bringing SHEPHERDS and wise men to worship.
Thank you for giving us all the BABY JESUS,
our GOD and KING.
Amen.

Song

'Ever since the world began'[33]

Plus

Suggestions for optional extras:

MUSIC   'Zachariah was a priest'[34]

---

33. Barry Hart, *Sing the day through*, Kevin Mayhew 2009.
34. Alison Carver, *Sing the day through*, Kevin Mayhew 2009.

Missing!
Mary and Joseph lose Jesus

The Plot

Jesus and his family go on a pilgrimage to Jerusalem with their whole village and thousands of other Jews. On the way home, Jesus goes missing and Mary and Joseph return to Jerusalem to look for him. They find him talking to the teachers in the Temple. They are cross with him for getting lost, but he wonders why they didn't know he'd be there – in the house of God, his Father. *(Luke 2:41-52)*

The Point

Jesus is the Son of God, but he also knows what it's like to be an ordinary child who gets into trouble.

Story

I've got a story for you today. If you want to hear it, shout, 'What's the story?'

Encourage all to shout: **What's the story?**

This story is called 'Missing!' and it's about a boy who gets lost. Can you put your hand up if you've ever got lost?

Invite responses.

Who found you again?

Invite one child to answer.

What did your parents do when you'd been found?

Invite another child to answer.

This is the story of when Jesus got lost. He was a bit bigger than you – he was twelve years old. Three times a year, he and his family and all the Jews in the area went on a pilgrimage to Jerusalem. The pilgrimages were special journeys to celebrate Jewish festivals. Can I have some volunteers to show us what Jesus' family might have looked like on their pilgrimage?

WHAT'S THE STORY?

> *Invite volunteers and pick one of the oldest, tallest boys to be Jesus, then four smaller boys to be his brothers and two girls to be his sisters. Invite two teachers to come and represent Mary and Joseph. Gather this family group together at the front of the assembly hall.*

Now, here are Jesus and his family. They are going to have to walk all the way to Jerusalem. The journey will take them about four days, so they'll be camping for three nights. Who has been on a camping trip?

> *Invite responses.*

What do you need to take with you when you're camping?

> *Invite responses and gather lots of suggestions.*

That's a lot of stuff! Jesus and his family had to carry the same sort of things: all the bits for their tent, as well as their bedding and everything they needed for their meals. I wonder whether our volunteers can imagine carrying all that stuff. The youngest children sometimes rode on the family's donkey when their legs got tired. I'll bet they asked their big brothers for piggy-backs, too.

> *Encourage your volunteers to mime carrying rugs, blankets, cooking pots, cloths for the tent etc. An older child might like to give a younger child a piggy-back if it's safe to do so.*

So this is what Jesus and his family looked like on their pilgrimage.

> *Applaud your volunteers and ask them to sit down.*

But it wasn't just Jesus and his family. If we were Jews in Jesus' home town of Nazareth, we would ALL be going on a pilgrimage to Jerusalem together. Imagine how full this hall would be if all our families were here with us! Imagine how much stuff we'd all be carrying between us! Imagine what fun it would be – like the biggest school trip ever. All your friends would be coming. Hands up if you'd ask your mum or dad whether you could walk with your friends, rather than sticking with your family!

> *Invite responses.*

That's certainly what Jesus did. He was a sensible big brother, so he was allowed. He walked with his friends, surrounded by huge crowds of neighbours, as all the Jews from Nazareth headed through the hills of Galilee, along the fertile valley of the River Jordan and up the steep, rocky road that led to Jerusalem. Jesus joked with his friends and picnicked with other people's parents along the way.

In the big city of Jerusalem, the crowds were even bigger and the noise was tremendous. Think of the crowds at a football match, or at a music festival, or in the shops when there's a sale: crowds like these filled all the streets in Jerusalem. Everyone shared a special meal with their families on the night of the festival; the next day, they headed to the Temple, where people called to each other in different languages and shouted over the noise of the animals which were being sold for sacrifice. After all the bustle and excitement, it was time to head home.

The folk from Nazareth gathered together and set off. The first part of the journey was a lot easier, as this time they were going downhill, through the rocky landscape around Jerusalem. They walked all day until it was time to set up camp for the night. Joseph put up the tent and Mary lit a fire. Jesus' brothers said goodbye to their friends and followed the smell of their mum's cooking. Soon it was dark, but Jesus still hadn't turned up. Where do you think he was?

Invite suggestions.

All those ideas occurred to Mary and Joseph. Mary stayed up waiting for Jesus, but when he still hadn't come back by the morning, she started to panic. Where on earth had he got to? No one had seen him all day: Mary and Joseph realised they'd have to go back to the city and look for their son.

They set off, worrying as they went that Jesus had been attacked, kidnapped or even killed. They couldn't find any trace of him along the road. In Jerusalem, they looked everywhere and asked everyone, 'Have you seen our boy, Jesus? He's 12 – about this tall.' How long do you think they spent looking for Jesus? How long was he lost for?

Invite suggestions.

Three days! Three days alone in the big city without his mum and dad! No wonder they were worried. Finally they went back to the Temple – and there he was, talking to the teachers and asking questions. People were saying to each other, 'What a wise young man! Look how much he understands, at such a young age!'

Mary and Joseph couldn't believe their eyes. Mary cried out, 'Son, why have you treated us like this? Look, your father and I have been worried sick! We've been looking everywhere for you!'

And Jesus replied, 'Why were you looking for me? Didn't you know I'd be here, in my Father's house?' Jesus thought it was obvious he'd be in God's house, as God was his Father. He didn't feel lost at all! The Bible doesn't tell us what Mary and Joseph said next. It just states that they didn't understand, and that they took Jesus back to Nazareth. That must have felt like an extra-long walk home. What do you think they said to each other on the way?

Invite responses.

The Point

Christians believe that Jesus is the Son of God: he reminded his mum and dad of that when he said that the Temple was his Father's house. In this story, he got lost and got into trouble, and this reminds us that he was also an ordinary child like all of you. He knows what it's like to grow up, to be a member of a family and – sometimes – to be shouted at by cross parents. Jesus knows what it's like to be us, so we can always pray to God and know he'll understand.

WHAT'S THE STORY?

The Prayer

For our prayers today, we're going to use some actions to help us think about how God knows what it's like to be us. When I say 'ME', I want you all to point at yourselves. When I say 'YOU' to God, I want you all to point up to heaven. Let's practise: 'I'm ME!'

Everyone points at themselves.

You're YOU!

Everyone points up.

Let us pray.

Son of God,
I'm ME!
Thank YOU for being YOU,
and knowing what it's like to be ME, too.
Amen.

Song

'If I were a butterfly'[35]

Plus

Suggestions for optional extras:

IT   Show a picture of the Temple mount in Jerusalem.

MUSIC   'In a little town one day'[36]

---

[35]. *Anglican Hymns Old & New*, Kevin Mayhew 2008.
[36]. Val Hawthorne, *Sing the day through*, Kevin Mayhew 2009.

Wet, Wet, Wet
The story of Jesus' baptism

> ### The Plot
> Jesus is baptised in the River Jordan by John the Baptist, along with thousands of people. When he emerges from the water, a heavenly dove lands on him and a voice from heaven says, 'This is my beloved Son, with whom I am well pleased.'
>
> *(Matthew 3:13-17)*
>
> ### The Point
> No one is left in any doubt about who Jesus is, and his baptism marks the beginning of his public ministry. Baptism is a fresh start.

Story

I've got a story for you today. If you want to hear it, shout, 'What's the story?'

Encourage all to shout: **What's the story?**

This story is called 'Wet, Wet, Wet', and it's the story of when Jesus and lots of other people got baptised. In churches today, we have baptisms, which are sometimes called Christenings. Who has been to one of those?

Invite responses.

What happens at a baptism in church these days?

Invite a child to describe a baptism.

In Jesus' time, lots of people got baptised when they were grown-ups. What's more, they didn't just get a little splash of water in church: they were dunked in the river! Let's try to imagine what that was like. Can I have a volunteer please?

Select a tall child.

Let's imagine you're a person from Jesus' village and you're going to get baptised in the River Jordan. We'll call you Simeon *(or Rachel)*. Now, I need two volunteers to be the river.

WHAT'S THE STORY?

> *Invite responses and choose two volunteers to squat facing each other, in front of your baptism volunteer, with their hands on each other's shoulders. Their arms represent the river water, which at the moment only reaches your volunteer's knees.*

Here's the river. At the moment, it only comes up to your knees, but you've got to wade deeper if you're going to get baptised. Out there, in the middle of the river, is a man called John the Baptiser. He's waiting for you.

> *Encourage your baptism volunteer to walk on the spot, while your river volunteers begin to stand up, so that their arms – representing the water level – now reach your volunteer's waist.*

The river's getting deeper and colder – you're nearly there!

> *Your baptism volunteer continues to walk on the spot, while your river volunteers stand up, so that the water level now reaches your volunteer's chest.*

When you're out in the middle of the river, John the Baptiser asks you if you're sorry for everything you've ever done wrong, and whether you're ready to make a fresh start. You say 'YES!' So, Simeon *(or Rachel)*, are you sorry and ready to make a fresh start?

> *Encourage the volunteer to reply:* **YES!** *Ask the river volunteers to raise their arms right up and over the baptism volunteer's head, so that he/she comes up for air between their arms.*

And that's it! Our newly baptised Simeon *(or Rachel)* is wet, wet, wet, but the baptism is a sign that all *his/her* sins have been washed away and *he/she* can start a new life.

> *Give all your volunteers a round of applause and ask them to sit down.*

John the Baptist, as we call him today, baptised thousands of people like this in the River Jordan. They queued all along the banks. One day, Jesus joined the end of the queue and waited patiently for his turn in the river. When John saw him, he said, 'I can't baptise you! You don't need forgiving: you haven't done anything wrong! You should be baptising *me*!'

But Jesus said, 'Just go with it. It's the right thing to do.'

So Jesus waded out into the middle of the river, just like our volunteer did. The water came up to his knees; then it got deeper and colder as it reached his waist and then his chest. He reached the middle of the river and John baptised him. The newly baptised Jesus was wet, wet, wet, and the baptism was a sign that he was ready to start a new life.

Just then, something amazing happened. The sky opened and a heavenly dove flew down. This wasn't an ordinary bird: everyone who saw how brightly it shone knew that it was God's Holy Spirit. It landed gently on Jesus, its wings touching his face like a blessing. Then a voice from heaven spoke, loud and soft at the same time: the voice said gently, 'This is my beloved Son. I am well pleased with him.'

The Point

When Jesus was baptised, God made a public announcement in front of all those people who were queuing to go in the river. He knew that they were waiting for their Saviour, God's Chosen One, so with the mysterious dove and the voice from heaven God said, 'This is him!' God introduced him to the crowds, and his baptism marked the beginning of his new, public life: he started his life's work of teaching and healing.

The Prayer

This story reminds us that we can all make a fresh start. After his baptism, Jesus began a new kind of work. All those people in the river said sorry for the things they had done wrong and made a new beginning. Whenever we say sorry, we can be forgiven and make a fresh start, too. For our prayers today, I want you to think of the things you want to say sorry for. Imagine they are like splodges of mud or paint on your hands: for example, I'm imagining a big splodge for something I wish I hadn't done and a little splodge for the unkind words I said when I was cross.

Let's take a moment to imagine that our hands are mucky with all the things we want to say sorry for.

Pause for a moment.

Now, when we say sorry to God, we know that he'll wash all these bad things away. So as we say sorry in our hearts, let's imagine that we're washing our hands clean under a stream of fresh water. Let us pray.

Rub your hands as if washing them and encourage everyone else to do the same.

Loving God,
may you wash us clean and give us a fresh start.
Amen.

Song

'Jesus taught his friends a prayer'[37]

Plus

Suggestions for optional extras:

IT — You could show a still from the baptism scene in the film, *'O Brother, Where Art Thou?'*[38], which gives a good impression of crowds at a river baptism.

MUSIC — 'One more step along the world I go'[39]

---

37. Val Hawthorne, *Sing the day through*, Kevin Mayhew 2009.
38. Universal Studios, 2000. This scene may be found under Scene selection: chapter 4 – Redemption.
39. *Anglican Hymns Old & New*, Kevin Mayhew 2008.

Deserted
Jesus in the wilderness and the start of Lent

The Plot

Jesus goes into the wilderness alone and fasts for forty days. The devil tempts him three times: he suggests Jesus turn some stones into bread; he dares Jesus to jump from a high place to test whether God will send angels to rescue him; finally, he offers all the wealth and power in the world if Jesus will worship him. Jesus turns down each temptation with words from the Bible and then the devil leaves him alone.

(Matthew 4:1-11)

The Point

During Lent, Christians remember the time Jesus spent in the wilderness.

Story

I've got a story for you today. If you want to hear it, shout, 'What's the story?'

Encourage all to shout: **What's the story?**

This story is called 'Deserted'. It's about Jesus and the time he spent alone in the desert. Now, Jesus' desert wasn't like a nice, sandy beach. It was hot, dry and empty. There were rocks, stones, steep cliffs and jagged ravines. People called it 'the wilderness': it scared them because wild animals lived there and strange things happened in the great, hot silence. Jesus went off alone into the wilderness for forty days: forty days of walking on dry stones under the hot sun, and forty nights of freezing desert air. He didn't have anything to eat, so he was tired and hungry.

One day, the devil found Jesus alone in the wilderness. He began to tempt Jesus to do wrong. Now, this next part of our story describes a struggle between Jesus, on one side, and the devil who is persuading, daring and tempting him, on the other. We'll call this bad guy 'the tempter'. I need your help in telling this bit, so I'll divide the hall in half.

Divide the assembly hall down the middle.

Everyone on this side, could you be Jesus in this story? And everyone on that side, could you be the tempter? I'll tell you all what to do when the time comes. Now, to begin with, the tempter saw how hungry Jesus was. He said, *(gloatingly)* 'Oooooh!'

Encourage the tempters to repeat: **Oooooh!**

'Oooooh!' said the tempter. 'You must be STARVING! Those lumps of stone over there really look like loaves of bread, don't they? I'll tell you what, Jesus, why don't you use your power to turn them into real bread? Then you could have something to eat. Come on, you're God's Son – you've got to keep your strength up.'

But Jesus said, 'NO!'

Encourage the Jesus side to repeat: **NO!**

Remember that big, strong 'NO!' because you might need it again. Then Jesus repeated some words from the Bible: 'People don't just need bread to live – they need God's word.'

The tempter didn't give up. He led Jesus up to a very high place and said, 'I dare you to jump off! It says in the Bible that God will send his angels to protect you – I dare you to see if that's true! Go on – JUMP!'

Encourage the tempters to repeat: **JUMP!**

But Jesus said, 'NO!'

Encourage the Jesus side to repeat: **NO!**

'NO!' said Jesus. 'It also says in the Bible, "Don't put God to the test!"'

Then the tempter showed Jesus an amazing view of many big cities spread out before him. He said, 'Look at all the money, fame and power there is in the world: it could all be yours if you worship me! Go on, you know you want it: MONEY! FAME! POWER!'

Encourage the tempters to repeat: **MONEY! FAME! POWER!**

But Jesus said, 'NO!'

Encourage the Jesus side to repeat: **NO!**

'NO!' said Jesus. 'The Bible says, "Worship God and no one else." Go away, you devil!' Finally the tempter gave up, and God sent angels to look after Jesus.

The Point

We are coming up to the time of year we call Lent, which is the forty days before Easter. During Lent, Christians remember this story of Jesus being tempted in the wilderness. The tempter offered him all the things that would have made his life comfortable: plenty to eat, lots of power and proof that he was being looked after by guardian angels. Every time he was tempted, Jesus said, 'NO!' and he relied on God.

WHAT'S THE STORY?

Many people, not just Christians, try to resist temptation during Lent by giving up something they enjoy, such as chocolate or sweets. We have a big party on Pancake Day, to use up all the sugary treats in the house, then Lent begins the next day. Giving things up for Lent reminds Christians to rely on God, and it can help all of us to see what we really need, and what we can do without.

The Prayer

For our prayers today, we'll have some quiet thinking time. Think about what you would struggle to do without for forty days: chocolate? Crisps? Your games console? The Internet? In a quiet moment now, think about giving something up and ask God, 'Do I really need it?' Let's be quiet and ask that question in our hearts.

Pause for a short time.

God of life and love,
during Lent, may we learn what we really need.
Amen.

Song

'Soon it will be pancake day'[40]

Plus

Suggestions for optional extras:

- **IT**   Show a picture of the Judean desert.
- **MUSIC**   'Lent is a time when we think of others'[41]

---

40. Denis O'Gorman, *Sing the day through*, Kevin Mayhew 2009.
41. Denis O'Gorman, *Sing the day through*, Kevin Mayhew 2009.

Gone Fishing
Jesus calls the disciples

The Plot

Jesus finds the fishermen – Simon Peter, Andrew, James and John – at the end of an unsuccessful fishing trip. He tells them to cast their nets one more time. Sceptical, they do so, and find that their nets are bursting with fish. They are amazed and somewhat alarmed at this bumper catch. Jesus tells them not to be afraid, because now they'll be catching people instead of fish. They drop everything and follow him.

(Luke 5:1-11)

The Point

These four fishermen were Jesus' first disciples. Their job was 'catching people' for God by encouraging them to follow Jesus, too. That's what they did, and the tons of fish they caught in this story represent the millions of Christians spread across the world today.

Story

I've got a story for you today. If you want to hear it, shout, 'What's the story?'

Encourage all to shout: **What's the story?**

This story is called 'Gone Fishing' and it's about two pairs of brothers who were partners in a small fishing business. Their names were Simon Peter and Andrew, James and John. Can I have some volunteers to be these four fishermen?

Choose four volunteers (boys or girls) and invite them to the front.

Now, these fishermen didn't use fishing rods. They used big fishing nets which they threw into the water. Can you all pretend that you're holding the edge of a big net?

Your volunteers mime holding the nets.

Now, to catch fish in these nets you need to throw them into the water – but keep hold of one edge, otherwise you'll lose the whole net! So first you need to gather up the net into your arms in a big bundle.

WHAT'S THE STORY?

Your volunteers do so.

Then you need to throw it as far out into the water as you can – remember to hold on to one edge.

Encourage them to mime casting the nets over the heads of the children in the front rows.

Now you have to wait and wait. Finally, when you think lots of fish might have swum into your nets, you pull them up to check. They'll be wet and heavy, so it's hard work.

Encourage them to mime pulling in the nets with great effort.

Oh no! There aren't any fish in these nets!

Encourage the volunteers to react with disappointment.

You'll have to keep trying, or you won't make any money today – fishing is the only way you make a living.

Encourage them to mime casting the nets again.

This is what Simon Peter, Andrew, James and John were doing one morning on the Sea of Galilee. They had been fishing all night, but hadn't caught a single thing. They were tired and fed up.

Encourage them to yawn, stretch and look fed up.

Then Jesus turned up on the beach. He was teaching an enormous crowd of people. When he'd finished, he said to Simon Peter, 'Here's what you need to do. Get in your boat, head for the deep water and let down your nets. Go on, catch some fish.'
   Simon Peter replied, 'But we haven't caught a thing all night!' He sighed, and Jesus just smiled at him. 'All right,' said Simon. 'If you say so, we'll give it a go.'
   So the fishermen got in their boats and rowed out to the deep water.

Encourage your volunteers to sit down in a row, sideways on, and mime rowing.

Then they threw in their nets. Careful now – if you stand up in a boat, it'll wobble!

Encourage your volunteers to mime getting shakily to their feet and then casting their nets.

Suddenly, out of the deep water rose thousands and thousands of fish. *(to everyone in the hall)* Can you hold up your hands and make them swim like fish?

Encourage the rest of the assembly hall to mime fish with their hands.

Just look at this enormous shoal of fish! They flashed silver and white as they streamed through the water. The fishermen began to haul in their nets and the fish swam even faster.

Encourage the fishermen to mime hauling in the heavy nets and everyone else to mime very wiggly fish.

The fishing nets weighed a ton. They had so many fish in them that they were beginning to break. All the fishermen pulled and heaved until their boats were so full of fish that they started to sink. PANIC! The fishermen rowed quickly back to shore *(encourage mime)* as the fish flopped and the water washed about in the boats. At last, they got back to the beach and the fish lay still.

Ask your fishermen to stand up and everyone else to put their hands down.

The fishermen were amazed and terrified by what had just happened. These fish were the catch of a lifetime, but why had Jesus done such an amazing thing for them? Simon Peter felt he didn't deserve it at all, so he told Jesus to leave him alone. Jesus looked at Simon Peter and the other fishermen. He smiled kindly. 'Don't be scared,' he said. 'From now on you'll be catching people, not fish.'

The fishermen looked at each other, then they looked at Jesus. The next moment, they did something very surprising that changed their lives for ever. They left all the fish in their nets, turned their backs on their boats and followed Jesus.

Invite everyone to applaud your volunteer fishermen and the shoal of fish.

The Point

Those four fishermen – Simon Peter, Andrew, James and John – were Jesus' first followers, or *disciples*. They dropped everything to do a new job: they had to 'catch people' for God by encouraging them to follow Jesus, too. That's what they spent the rest of their lives doing, and as a result more and more people followed Jesus. Now, remember the fish caught by the fishermen in our story today – the enormous catch we showed with our hands.

Encourage everyone to wave their hands like fish again.

We can think of those tons of fish as representing the two billion Christians spread across the world today – and that number grew from four fishermen who followed Jesus.

The Prayer

Jesus told his first disciples that they were going to catch people for God. This story reminds us that God's love is like a net that gathers everyone in, so that nobody gets left behind. For our prayers today, we'll use our hands to make a net full of fish. Can you spread your hands out like stars, then slide them together so that your fingers interlock?

WHAT'S THE STORY?

Demonstrate this action, palms down, so that your fingers point downwards. Then turn your hands palm up and encourage everyone to do the same.[42]

Now, with your hands facing upwards like this, can you wiggle all your fingers so that they look like fish caught in a net?

Encourage everyone to do this and continue as you pray.

Let us pray.

Loving God,
thank you for your love which gathers us all up
like fish in a net.
Thank you for remembering us all
so that nobody gets left behind.
Amen.

Song

'There are hundreds of sparrows'[43]

Plus

Suggestions for optional extras:

PROPS A large piece of fishing net or garden netting for the fishermen to cast.

MUSIC 'I can learn'[44]

---

[42]. The action is like the childhood rhyme which is accompanied by hand movements: 'Here's the church and here's the steeple, open the door and here's the people.' In this case, the 'people' are wriggling like fish.
[43]. *Anglican Hymns Old & New*, Kevin Mayhew 2008.
[44]. Alison Carver, *Sing the day through*, Kevin Mayhew 2009.

The Miracle Drink
Jesus turns water into wine

The Plot

Jesus is a guest at a wedding. The reception is in full swing when the wine starts to run out – a social calamity for the hosts! Jesus steps in and miraculously turns gallons of water into the finest wine. *(John 2:1-11)*

The Point

Jesus is the Son of God and he loves to give.

Story

I've got a story for you today. If you want to hear it, shout, 'What's the story?'

Encourage all to shout: **What's the story?**

This story is called 'The Miracle Drink'. It is told by a servant who knew Jesus. I'm going to play the part of the servant, so I need you to imagine that I'm wearing a rough, dirty tunic. I've got bare feet and a cloth tied around my head, to keep off the sun and to soak up the sweat. There's a lot of sweat because I'm a very hard-working servant. I fetch and carry for my master and mistress from dawn to midnight. This is my special story.

There's loads to do today. Lots of guests coming, kitchens full of food and mountains of dishes. Special occasions are always like this: the hosts get stressed and we servants have to do all the work. Mind you, this party is nothing compared to what happens when there's a wedding on. The celebrations last for a week! The whole village comes, and everyone brings along their cousins and second cousins from the nearby villages. And they bring their friends, and friends of friends, and – well, you get the picture. Quite a crowd. And they all need food and drink. When there's a wedding on, it's work, work, work for us servants and you can forget about sleep. Maybe you get a nap in the small hours when the guests have finally stopped dancing – but then they're up and wanting to wash and eat again.

The washing – that's the thing that wears me out the most. We Jews have strict laws about washing: the guests all need to wash when they wake up, and before they eat, and after they've eaten, so that's a lot of water. And that means trips to the well, back and forth. Every time, I have to lower a big bucket to the bottom of the well, haul it up again and fill a big water carrier. Then I heave the water onto my shoulders, carry it inside and empty the lot into the massive stone jars we use for storage. These water jars are like – *this* big. *(Use your hands to suggest a water jar about the size of a domestic wheelie bin.)* Then I have to reach up and draw some water out of the jar every time someone needs a wash – and there's always someone. Before long, I'm scraping the bottom of the jar and it's back to the well again.

I need to show you just how big these water jars are: can I have some volunteers?

Choose five children and bring them to the front. Ask them to stand in a tight, inward-facing circle with their arms around each other's shoulders. If the circle is not tall enough (it needs to be about chest-high to you) ask the children to stretch their arms up to form the neck of the storage jar.

There – imagine a stone jar which is *this* wide and *this* tall! Imagine how much water this jar holds! Remember this jar, because there are six of them in my story.

Applaud your volunteers and ask them to sit down.

Stone jars full of water: they're all I ever see at weddings! I certainly never thought there could be anything special about them. But one wedding changed that forever. I'll never forget it. It was one of the biggest, noisiest, happiest weddings the town of Cana had ever seen. We servants were rushed off our feet, bringing out more and more food, filling wine glasses and then refilling them. Can you all make a noise like lots of people at a party?

Encourage a big, rowdy noise, then signal for quiet.

Imagine a noisy, happy party which lasted for a week! But after four days, we servants started to get worried. The wine was running low. We'd served up the best stuff first, but by now we were down to last year's sour grape juice – and it was still disappearing fast. At this rate, I thought, we're going to run out! Unheard of. It would bring such shame on my master's house if he let his guests down like that. People would never let him forget it. So we told the steward in charge of wine, and he told us to make it last as best we could, but by the fifth day there was no way round it. The wine had run out. We tried to keep it quiet, to give us some time while we thought of a way out of this mess, but word started to leak out. I heard whispers among the guests, and then a quiet little woman came into the servant's area. She pointed towards a young man standing on the edge of the crowd and told us, 'That's my son. Do whatever he tells you.'

Well, we weren't too impressed, I can tell you. Some bloke from the next village? Who was he to order us around? But he walked past us and looked into the stone water jars – empty, again. He turned round and said, 'Fill the jars with water.' All six? I thought. Easier said than done! Well, he was a guest and I had to do as he asked, but – there was something about him. I didn't understand what he was up to, or how this was going to help with the wine situation, but he seemed very *sure*. Doing what he said just seemed like the right thing to do, so I shouted for all the other servants and we headed out to the well. There and back, there and back, it took us the best part of an hour, but in the end we filled all six water jars to the brim. I turned round after I'd emptied in the last load and that young man was standing right behind me.

'Now draw some out and take it to the wine steward,' he said. I still didn't have a clue what he was doing – did the steward want to wash his hands? But I dipped my jug into the water jar which I'd just finished filling and – well, you'll never believe it. None of us could, but it's true: that water had turned into wine. All of it! All six stone jars full! And not just any old wine, either. When I took some to the steward to taste, he rolled his eyes and smacked his lips and sighed, 'Now that's what I call fine wine! Where has the bridegroom been hiding this, then? I've never tasted anything like it!'

We rushed round and filled everyone's glasses then, and that wedding party was always remembered as the one that saved the best wine 'til last. But those of us who were there when the miracle happened – those of us who fetched the water with our own hands – we remember it for another reason. That was the day we saw God's power in his Son, Jesus of Nazareth. From then on, nothing could shake my belief in him, and I've told my story to anyone who would listen.

Song

'We've a sing-along song'[45]

The Point

Today we've heard the story of Jesus' first miracle. It was the first time he showed that he had God's power, and the hard-working servants in our story were the first to understand what had happened. We can remember this story with a short rhyme: *(encourage the children to repeat each line after you)*

They poured in water,

he poured out wine,

Jesus proved his power divine.

Repeat the rhyme all together.

The Prayer

We are going to use our hands to help us pray today. Can you make a bowl with your hands, as if you're trying to scoop up water?

Demonstrate with your hands and encourage everyone to do the same.

Our story today showed how God loves to give. He gave the wedding guests more fine wine than they could drink! Let's be quiet for a moment. Close your eyes and hold out your hands, then silently ask God for something you need.

---

45. Val Hawthorne, *Sing the day through*, Kevin Mayhew 2009.

WHAT'S THE STORY?

Pause.

Amen.

We don't know when or how God will answer our prayers – he might surprise us, just as he surprised the wedding guests in our story. For now, we'll have to wait and see.

Plus

Suggestions for optional extras:

IT Picture of giant stone water jars.

COSTUME A head-cloth, secured with a simple tie.

MUSIC 'In this world it's not hard to spot'[46]

---

46. Barry Hart, *30 Catchy New Assembly Songs*, Kevin Mayhew 2009.

The All-You-Can-Eat Picnic
Jesus feeds the five thousand

The Plot
Thousands of people follow Jesus round the shores of Lake Galilee. By the end of the day, everyone is hungry but no one has brought any food with them – apart from one small boy. He gives his five bread rolls and two small fish to Jesus, who shares them with the crowds. Everyone eats until they are full and the disciples collect twelve baskets of leftovers.

(John 6:1-14)

The Point
God will provide – but we have to help, by sharing what we have.

Story

I've got a story for you today. If you want to hear it, shout, 'What's the story?'

Encourage all to shout: **What's the story?**

This story is called 'The All-You-Can-Eat Picnic' and it's about a lot of hungry people. Let's set the scene. Imagine that you've come into school this morning and I've stood up to tell you this important news: I'm afraid there has been a power cut in the school kitchen, and the lorry that was going to deliver all the food has broken down. So there will be no school dinners today! And I'm sorry to say this, but all the packed lunches have been eaten by hungry teachers who forgot to have breakfast. There's just one packed lunch left – and it's got to feed the whole school at lunch time! Now, who can remember what was in their packed lunch today?

Invite responses and ask one child to list the contents of his/her packed lunch. Repeat the list so that everyone can hear.

Luckily, yours is the one packed lunch that is left! So that's all we have to share between us for lunch. How are we going to manage?

Invite suggestions.

It's a challenge, isn't it? Luckily, none of us will go hungry today, because in fact the school kitchens are full of food and so are your packed lunch boxes. What a relief! But Jesus had to face the challenge of feeding lots of hungry people with just one packed lunch. This is what happened.

WHAT'S THE STORY?

Jesus was healing sick people everywhere he went. If you were blind, he cured you. If you'd broken your leg, he cured you. Even if you'd been paralysed from birth, he cured you, too. No wonder he was followed by thousands of fans wherever he went.

One day, the crowds followed Jesus right round to the other side of Lake Galilee. There were about five thousand people and it was a long way – some walked nearly fifteen miles! They followed Jesus to hear him talk, to watch him heal and to be made better themselves. They walked all day; as they reached Jesus the sun was getting lower in the sky. It was way past lunch time and tummies were beginning to rumble. Can you hold your tummies as if you're really hungry?

Encourage everyone to clutch their stomach.

Children said to their mums, 'What is there to eat? I'm STARVING!'

Jesus heard what the children said and he asked his disciples a question: 'Where can we buy some food for all these hungry people?'

One disciple said, 'We can't afford to feed this lot! It would cost more than we earn in half a year! Even then, they'd only get a mouthful each.'

Another disciple said, 'No one's brought any food apart from that boy over there. He's got a packed lunch. But it's only five bread rolls and two fish – that won't go far with this many people!'

Jesus called the boy over and asked, 'Please will you share your packed lunch with us?'

The boy replied, 'Er – OK then. Here you are.'

Jesus took the bread and the fish and said a prayer. He broke the bread rolls into pieces and popped a piece of fish in each one. Then he started to hand round the food. Let's imagine that all of us here today are the five thousand hungry people sitting down on the grass beside Lake Galilee. If I give everyone in the front row a handful of bread and fish, can you pretend to break it in half and pass some to the person sitting behind you?

Mime handing out the bread and fish and encourage everyone to share some with the person sitting behind them.

Now, miraculously, the people in the second row have got just as much bread and fish as the people in the front row! So can you each share some of yours with the person sitting behind you?

Encourage more mimed sharing of food.

Now, the front two rows can start eating their bread and fish. Delicious! Meanwhile, the rest of you, keep passing the food back: when you get yours, pass half of it to the person behind you and then start eating. Don't forget the teachers! They're hungry too.

Encourage everyone to mime sharing food and eating it, until the imaginary food has been passed right around the assembly hall.

This is what happened at Jesus' picnic: everyone kept passing round the food, and the more they passed it round, the more food there seemed to be, until those five bread rolls and two fish fed five thousand people, and they were all full! When Jesus sent his disciples to clear up the leftovers – the crusts and the fish bones – they filled twelve baskets! When people realised that it was a miracle, they said to each other, 'This Jesus is really special – he's God's Chosen One we've been waiting for!'

The Point

In the Bible, this all-you-can-eat picnic is called 'The feeding of the five thousand'. Jesus fed all those hungry people, and his miracle shows that God gives us what we need – but we have to do our bit, too. What if that little boy had refused to share his packed lunch? What if Jesus and his disciples had eaten it all themselves? Jesus made the miracle happen, but it all started with a little boy who was kind enough to share. We all need to practise sharing, because who knows? One day our sharing might help something amazing happen.

The Prayer

In church, Christians practise sharing when they do something called 'sharing the Peace'. This is when everyone shakes hands with each other and says, 'Peace be with you'. It reminds everyone to share God's good things – like peace and love and kindness – with whoever they meet. Today we're going to share the Peace with each other. I'd like you to turn to the people sitting next to you and shake each other's hands. Say to each other, 'Peace be with you.'

Share the Peace with a child in the front row and encourage everyone else to do the same.

We'll end with a special word that means 'so be it': it means 'may what we've asked for actually happen' – may there really be peace with us all. That special word is 'Amen'. Let's say it together: **Amen**.

Song

'5 0 0 0 + hungry folk'[47]

Plus

Suggestions for optional extras:

PROPS You could have a filled school packed lunch box with you and hold up the contents; you could even use five brown bread rolls and two cooked sprats as a visual aid.

MUSIC 'Go and grab a cook book'[48]

---

47. *Anglican Hymns Old & New*, Kevin Mayhew 2008.
48. Barry Hart, *Sing the day through*, Kevin Mayhew 2009.

In Charge
Jesus heals the centurion's servant

The Plot

A Roman centurion's beloved slave falls ill and he asks for Jesus' help, but when he sees Jesus heading to his house, he has second thoughts. He sends a message to say that he doesn't deserve Jesus' personal assistance: all he asks Jesus to do is say the word, like an officer giving an order, and his slave will get better. Jesus is amazed by the centurion's faith and heals the slave.

(Luke 7:1-10)

The Point

The Roman centurion understands authority: he recognises that Jesus is the Son of God and he is in charge. His story reminds us that God is the boss.

Story

Place a chair at the front of the assembly hall.

I've got a story for you today. If you want to hear it, shout, 'What's the story?'

Encourage all to shout: **What's the story?**

This story is called 'In Charge' and it's about who is the boss. In Jesus' time, the big boss was the Roman Emperor. Can you put your hands up if you have learned about the Romans?

Invite responses.

As you all know, the Roman Empire had a powerful army. Can I have six volunteers to be Roman soldiers, please?

Invite six volunteers forward and line them up in front of you. Using real or mimed costumes and props, dress them up as each of the following as you name them.

Now, Roman soldiers were very clear about who was in charge. Top of the heap was the Roman emperor – the most powerful man of all. He wore a golden crown of leaves and a rich cloak.

Crown him and drape a cloak over his shoulders.

IN CHARGE – JESUS HEALS THE CENTURION'S SERVANT

The emperor chose his legionary commanders. They wore fine armour.

Give the next child a breastplate.

Each legion of the Roman army had senior centurions. They carried strong swords.

Give the next child a sword.

The senior centurions were in charge of the ordinary centurions, who carried weapons of their own.

Give the next child a dagger.

The centurions gave orders to their seconds-in-command: these are the orders, written on a scroll.

Unroll the scroll then roll it up again and give it to the next child.

The seconds-in-command read the orders and told the ordinary soldiers what to do.

Ask the second-in-command to give the scroll to the last child.

The ordinary soldier, with his shield and sword, defended the Roman Empire.

Give the last child a shield and sword.

Our story today is about a man who has spent his life in the army, taking orders from people above him and giving orders to people below him. He is the centurion.

Ask the centurion to step forward.

If you asked him his name and rank, he'd answer, *(briskly, like a soldier on parade)* 'Marcus Fabius Strabo, SIR! Commander of the third century of the tenth cohort. I'm in charge of the Roman army in Galilee: here to enforce Roman rule and keep the peace, SIR!' I want you to remember this centurion as I tell you his story.

Applaud your volunteers and ask them to sit down.

The centurion was a good man. Although he was in charge of the Roman army in Galilee, he was kind to the locals. He got on well with the Jewish people and he even built them a special place, called a synagogue, in which they could worship God. The centurion lived with a slave whom he loved and completely relied upon. The slave was called Afer and he was a cross between a butler and a best friend. Can I have a volunteer to be this faithful servant?

Bring forward a volunteer.

WHAT'S THE STORY?

This is Afer. He did everything for his boss, the centurion. If he wanted grapes, Afer brought him a bunch; if he wanted his armour, Afer polished it for him, and if he needed a letter writing, Afer wrote it for him. Afer worked hard but he had a good life: he was never cold, never hungry and his boss always treated him kindly. In fact, the centurion often said, 'Afer, you're my right-hand man. What would I do without you?'

One terrible day, Afer fell ill.

Encourage your volunteer to sink into a chair and look ill.

He was iller than that – he looked as if he were going to die.

Encourage your volunteer to look very ill indeed.

The centurion was desperate. None of his Roman medicine made any difference, so he sent a message to his friends, the Jews. The message was, 'Please ask Jesus to come and make my slave better!' Can I have a volunteer to be Jesus, please?

Choose a volunteer in the back row of the assembly hall and ask him/her to stand up.

The Jews took the centurion's message to Jesus. Here it is.

Pass a scroll – mimed or real – to a child in the first row and ask him/her to pass it back, and so on, until the message reaches Jesus.

Meanwhile, Afer the slave felt worse and worse. *(encourage more acting)* He was in terrible pain and close to death. Jesus was still a long way off, surrounded by crowds, and the centurion waited impatiently for him to arrive. Suddenly, the centurion saw Jesus heading towards his house, surrounded by the Jews. He looked down at himself in all his Roman uniform and thought, 'What am I doing?' He quickly sent Jesus another message.

Mime scribbling on a scroll and pass it to a child in the front row, who passes it back to Jesus as before.

The message said: 'Lord, I'm not one of your people and I don't deserve to have you in my house. But I'm a soldier who is used to giving orders. When I tell someone to do something, he does it. So all you need to do is give the order, and I know my servant will get better.'

Jesus was amazed. He gave the word and in the centurion's house, Afer the slave suddenly felt better. In fact, all the pain had gone and he was completely well again!

Encourage Afer to recover quickly and stand up.

Jesus said to the Jews, 'Look, you lot – this Roman soldier gets it! He understands that God's in charge and I'm his Son! That's the kind of faith *you* need to have.'

The centurion was full of joy to see his servant well again, and Afer had never felt better!

Applaud your volunteers and ask them to sit down.

IN CHARGE – JESUS HEALS THE CENTURION'S SERVANT

The Point

We began our story by looking at a line-up of the Roman army, with the Emperor at the top and the ordinary soldier at the bottom. Everyone (apart from the Emperor) had to follow orders, so the Roman centurion understood what being in charge meant. He recognised that Jesus was in charge and his story reminds us that God is the boss – no one is more important than him.

The Prayer

When we pray to God, we show that he's the boss in different ways. Sometimes we kneel or bow our heads: it's a bit like bowing or curtseying when you meet a king or queen. Sometimes we call God 'Father' because we're like his children. These things remind us that God is in charge of us and he looks after us, too. So for our prayers today, we will kneel down or bow our heads as we pray.

Pause while everyone gets into position.

Father God,
you're the boss.
Take charge of our lives
and take care of us.
Amen.

Song

'So good, so kind'[49]

Plus

Suggestions for optional extras:

IT As an introduction, play the *Horrible Histories* clip: 'Surviving in the Roman Army.'[50]

PROPS A piece of rich fabric, ideally red or purple; any items of Roman armour or weaponry[51]; two scrolls of paper.

MUSIC 'Dear Father, who is in heaven'[52]

---

49. Barry Hart, *30 Catchy New Assembly Songs*, Kevin Mayhew 2009.
50. This one-minute clip is available on YouTube – search for 'Horrible Histories Surviving in the Roman Army'. It makes the point perfectly, as well as being historically accurate and very funny.
51. You may have items left over from a project on the Romans; alternatively, English Heritage outlets sell toy swords and Roman armour.
52. Alison Carver, *Sing the day through*, Kevin Mayhew 2009.

Get Up!
Jesus heals the paralysed man

The Plot

Jesus is teaching people in a house in Capernaum and drawing enormous crowds. When four friends bring a paralysed man for healing, they can't even get through the door, so they make a hole in the roof and lower him down right in front of Jesus. Jesus forgives the man and heals him, too: he stands up and walks home, to everyone's amazement.

(Mark 2:1-12)

The Point

Jesus is the Son of God: he acts with God's authority and has the power to help and heal.

Story

I've got a story for you today. If you want to hear it, shout, 'What's the story?'

Encourage all to shout: **What's the story?**

This story is called 'Get Up!' and it is about a man who couldn't walk. He was paralysed and spent his days lying on his sleeping mat, wishing there was someone who could make him well again. His friends brought him rumours of a man called Jesus: they said he was a bloke who could cure people of all sorts of terrible illnesses, just by touching them and saying a few words. The paralysed man hoped it was true, and do you know what? It was! Ordinary people loved Jesus and couldn't wait to see what he'd do next. He tried to avoid publicity, but soon he was famous. Wherever he went, there were always crowds and they made a big noise. Can you cheer like Jesus' crowds of fans?

Encourage everyone to cheer.

Jesus couldn't walk into town without being mobbed. When he arrived, word spread fast in the market place: 'He's back! He's here! Jesus is here! Come and be cured! Come and see!' I wonder if we can make a noise like that excited crowd. I'm going to divide you into three sections.

Divide the assembly hall into three sections and give them each a line to say.

GET UP! – JESUS HEALS THE PARALYSED MAN

I want you to say, 'He's here!' I want you to say, 'It's Jesus!' and I want you to say, 'Come and see!' Now, let's say our lines together over and over again so that we sound like those excited crowds around Jesus.

Encourage everyone to say their lines together, then signal for the noise to stop.

The man who couldn't walk – remember him? – heard all this excited noise and reckoned this was his chance to be cured by Jesus. He asked four of his friends to carry him on his sleeping mat to Jesus' house. Now, Jesus was at home but there were so many people, the house was full to bursting and no one could get near the front door. Shoving and elbowing their way through the crowds, the four friends carried the man on his sleeping mat. The only place left anywhere near Jesus was the flat roof of his house. With a great heaving, they made it up the steps which ran up the outside wall. Once on the roof, they could see the huge crowd pressing around the little house. They felt as if they were on an island in a sea of people. Through the roof's thin tiles, they could hear Jesus talking. So close! One man lifted up a loose tile. He peeped through and saw every head turned one way. Jesus was teaching, and he was right underneath them. Suddenly the four friends had an idea. They took their strong fishermen's knives and starting prising up the roof tiles; then they began cutting a hole in the ceiling, sending lumps of plaster and wood into the room below. Can you all stamp your feet, to make a sound like bits of falling roof?

Encourage everyone to stamp their feet.

Jesus heard the noise and stopped talking. He looked up through the hole in his roof and saw four hopeful faces looking down at him. He nodded at them, and the men started to lower their friend down on his sleeping mat; more strong arms took the weight and laid the man gently on the floor in front of Jesus. Jesus smiled up at the men on the roof and then turned to their friend. He said, 'Son, your sins are forgiven.' At these words, there was a gasp of surprise. Can you all gasp as if you're really shocked?

Encourage everyone to gasp.

It was the religious types from the Temple who were shocked. 'How can he say that?' they asked each other. 'Who can forgive sins apart from God? Who does this Jesus think he is?'

Jesus said to them, 'Which is easier – to say to this paralysed man, "Your sins are forgiven", or to tell him to get up and walk? Watch this – I'm going to show you that I'm working with God's power here.' He turned to the paralysed man: 'You – get up! Pick up your bed and walk home.' At first the man looked terrified. Then his legs twitched, and he stretched, then slowly got to his feet. The crowd held its breath as he picked up his bed and walked towards the door, a grin spreading across his face with every step he took. Everyone cheered!

Encourage everyone to cheer.

His friends on the roof cheered loudest of all. Some people were speechless; others cried out and praised God. Many turned to their neighbours and said excitedly, 'Wow! We've never seen anything like this!' Can you all cheer and clap, as if you've just seen an amazing miracle?

Encourage everyone to cheer and applaud.

The Point

When Jesus healed the paralysed man, he proved to a huge crowd that he was God's Son, because he could use God's power to do good. This miracle reminds us that God sent Jesus to help people and make them better.

The Prayer

When we know someone who needs help, we can pray for them. God may not help them in the way we expect, but he will always hear our prayer. We're going to be quiet for a short time now as we remember the people we know who need help. Let us pray.

Pause for a short time of silence.

Lord, please use your power to help and heal.
Amen.

Song

'Where there is shouting'[53]

Plus

Suggestions for optional extras:

MUSIC   'Sometimes we might say words'[54]

---

[53]. Alison Carver, *Sing the day through*, Kevin Mayhew 2009.
[54]. Alison Carver, *Sing the day through*, Kevin Mayhew 2009.

Wake Up!
Jesus brings Lazarus back from the dead

The Plot

Jesus' friend Lazarus is dying. Instead of rushing to help, Jesus waits two days and then sets off. He arrives to find that Lazarus has died and was buried four days earlier. His sisters, Martha and Mary, are grieving for their brother and angry with Jesus for not healing him. They open the grave and Jesus calls Lazarus: the dead man comes back to life and lots of witnesses start believing in Jesus. *(John 11:1-46)*

The Point

Jesus is stronger than death: here he resurrects Lazarus, and after his death on the cross he himself is resurrected. Christians believe in life after death.

Story

I've got a story for you today. If you want to hear it, shout, 'What's the story?'

Encourage all to shout: **What's the story?**

This story is called 'Wake Up!' In fact, these are the two most powerful words in the story, and I'm going to need you all to say them with me. After three, let's say, 'Wake up!'

Count to three and encourage everyone to say: **Wake Up!**

That's OK, but it's not loud enough. In this story, those words need to be shouted loudly enough to wake the dead! Let's try again.

Count to three and encourage everyone to shout: **WAKE UP!**

Now listen out for the moment in our story when we need to shout those words. This story begins with one of Jesus' best friends. He was a man called Lazarus, and Jesus loved him. In fact, Jesus was close to the whole family: Lazarus lived with his sisters, Martha and Mary, and Jesus loved spending time at their house. He'd drop in for some food, or he'd stay the night, and Lazarus, Martha and Mary were always pleased to see him. You know how it is with best friends.

One day, Martha and Mary sent Jesus an urgent message. It said, 'Lazarus is sick – come soon!' Well, what would you do if your friend was ill?

WHAT'S THE STORY?

Invite responses.

Do you know what Jesus did? Nothing. Although he loved Lazarus and his sisters, he stayed exactly where he was for two more days! Then he set off on the long journey to Bethany, where the family lived.

When Jesus reached the road to Lazarus' house, he heard a strange noise: it was the sound of lots of people crying. Can you all make a crying noise?

Encourage everyone to do so.

That's what Jesus heard. He knew then that Lazarus had died, because in those days when there was a funeral, everyone in the village came, and people cried out loud together with the family. When Jesus heard the noise, he was really upset. He started crying, too. Then Martha and Mary came towards him, very sad and cross, and they said to Jesus, 'If you'd been here, our brother wouldn't have died!'

Jesus hugged the two sisters and they all cried together. Then he said: 'I am the resurrection and the life. Anyone who believes in me – even if they die – will live. Where have you buried him?'

Together they walked to Lazarus' grave. It wasn't a hole in the ground: it was a cave, and there was an enormous stone rolled across the entrance. Jesus said, 'Take away the stone.'

Martha replied, 'What?! But he's been dead for four days! There's a really bad smell in there!'

'Take away the stone,' Jesus insisted, 'and see what God will do.' So all the villagers gathered round and helped to roll away the huge boulder. Can you all make a noise as if you're moving something really heavy? Let's say, 'HEAVE!'

Encourage everyone to say: **HEAVE!** *together, as if struggling with a heavy weight.*

When the stone was rolled back, the bad smell of a dead body was strong enough to make your eyes water. Everyone held their noses or covered their mouths as if they were trying not to be sick. Can you all pretend you're trying not to breathe in a horrible smell?

Encourage everyone to do so.

Jesus looked up to heaven and said a prayer. Then he walked straight up to the entrance of the dark cave. He took a deep breath and shouted, 'Lazarus! WAKE UP!' His voice was so powerful, and there were so many echoes around the cave, that it sounded like a whole crowd of voices, shouting loudly enough to wake the dead.[55] So can we all shout 'WAKE UP!' together?

After a count of three, encourage everyone to shout: **WAKE UP!**

There was silence. Everyone peered into the gloomy cave and waited.

---

55. For convincing Biblical evidence of how Jesus' voice is described here, see Lucy Winkett, *Our Sound Is Our Wound*, Continuum 2010, pp 100-101.

Pause and hold the silence for a moment, then point and shout loudly enough to make people jump.

LOOK! There was Lazarus! He was still wrapped up like a mummy, but he was alive! He walked out of the tomb and into Jesus' arms. After a moment of stunned silence, everyone cheered.

Encourage everyone to cheer.

People rushed off to tell their friends about the miracle they had seen, and some reported the facts to the priests in Jerusalem. They used the big word '*resurrection*', which means 'coming back from the dead.' They remembered what Jesus said to Martha and Mary: 'I am the resurrection and the life. Anyone who believes in me – even if they die – will live.'

The Point

It's natural to be sad when someone dies. Jesus was so sad in today's story that he cried – even though he knew the story would have a happy ending. He brought Lazarus back from the dead and later, after he'd died on the cross, Jesus himself came back to life, too. This is known as the Resurrection. It's the reason Christians believe in life after death: as Jesus said in today's story, anyone who believes in him – even if they die – will live.

The Prayer

The story of Lazarus reminds us that we will always be sad when someone dies, and there will always be tears, but death isn't the end. Let's close our eyes for a prayer.

Living God,
cry with us when we are sad,
laugh with us when we are happy.
May we always live life with you.
Amen.

Song

'Times change'[56]

Plus

Suggestions for optional extras:

MUSIC 'Yesterday, today, for ever'[57]

---

56. Barry Hart, *Sing the day through*, Kevin Mayhew 2009.
57. *Anglican Hymns Old & New*, Kevin Mayhew 2008.

Man Overboard!
Jesus walks on the waves

The Plot

One evening, Jesus tells his disciples to row across the Sea of Galilee. A storm blows up and batters their boat. In the small hours of the morning, Jesus walks across the water to his disciples. At first they think he is a ghost, but he reassures them and tells Peter to walk across the waves towards him. Peter has a go, but he's scared of the storm and starts to sink. Jesus saves him, they get into the boat and the wind drops. All the disciples are now convinced he is the Son of God. *(Matthew 14:22-33)*

The Point

Peter needed to focus on Jesus, not the storm. This story is about holding on to faith in spite of the difficulties we may face in life.

Story

I've got a story for you today. If you want to hear it, shout, 'What's the story?'

Encourage all to shout: **What's the story?**

This story is called 'Man Overboard!' and it takes place on a huge lake. It's called Lake Galilee and it's no duck pond: it would take you six hours to swim across it and when a storm blows in, waves three metres high crash into the shore. One day, after Jesus had been teaching people on the far side of Lake Galilee, he went off on his own to pray and sent his disciples back across the lake in their boat. It was a strong boat and they were big fishermen, but even so it was difficult to row all that way. Can you all pretend that you're rowing a boat? It's hard work!

Mime strenuous rowing and encourage everyone to join in where they are sitting.

Before long, the sun began to set and it got darker and colder out on the water. By the time the disciples were in the middle of the lake, storm clouds covered the moon and a fierce wind was blowing hard at them. Can you all make a *swoooosh* like a strong wind?

Encourage everyone to make the sound of the wind.

MAN OVERBOARD! – JESUS WALKS ON THE WAVES

The wind whipped up big waves which battered the boat. In your rows, can you all hold hands with your neighbours and move your arms up and down to make rolling waves? Let's turn this whole hall into a stormy sea!

Encourage wave movements.

The poor disciples fought against the wind and waves all night. Just before dawn, they spotted a man not far away from the boat. He was walking on the water! Someone yelled, 'It's a ghost!' and everyone screamed! Could I have a volunteer to be this mysterious stranger in the middle of the lake?

Choose a volunteer in the middle of the assembly hall and ask him/her to stand up where they are. Encourage everyone else to continue the wave movements.

The man said, 'It's me – Jesus! Don't be frightened.'
Then Peter stood up in the boat. Can I have another volunteer to be Peter?

Choose a volunteer near the front and ask him/her to stand up and face Jesus.

Peter was very brave. He said, 'Lord, if it's really you, tell me to walk across the water to where you are!'
Jesus replied, 'Come on then, Peter.' Well, Peter tried. He stepped out of the boat and balanced on the first wave. He fixed his eyes on Jesus and took a step forward. But then he noticed how strong the wind was and how wild the waves were and he was really frightened. Can you make a noise like the wind and keep moving your arms like the waves?

Encourage everyone to renew their wind- and wave-making efforts.

Peter started to sink.

Encourage the people around Peter to stand up and raise their waving arms towards his head.

Peter's friends shouted, 'Man overboard!'

Encourage everyone to shout: **Man overboard!**

Jesus reached out his hand and caught him.

Encourage your Jesus volunteer to stretch out his hand towards Peter.

Jesus said, 'Where's your faith, Peter? Why didn't you believe?' Together they stepped back into the boat and sat down.

Encourage your volunteers to sit down.

WHAT'S THE STORY?

Immediately the wind dropped and the sea was calm. Everyone in the boat worshipped Jesus, saying, 'You really are the Son of God!'

Applaud your volunteers.

The Point

Peter tried hard to believe that he could walk across the waves. At first, he concentrated on Jesus, but when he looked at the storm, he was so frightened that he started to sink. His story shows what it's like to believe in God: we may try hard to concentrate on Jesus, but it's easy to get scared by the difficulties we all face in life, which feel like stormy waves that are drowning us. Whenever we're worried by problems and dangers, let's try to remember Jesus' words to his terrified friends in the boat: 'It's me – Jesus! Don't be frightened.'

The Prayer

For our prayers today, we'll use our hands to make waves like the ones in our story. I'd like you to spread your hands flat in front of you, palms down, and lace your fingers together. Then roll your hands and arms like the waves on the sea.

Demonstrate this undulating action at waist level.

Think about the wind and the waves that scared Peter in our story, and as you make waves with your hands, think about the things that are worrying you. Sometimes those worries can get bigger *(move your hands to chest level)* and deeper *(move your hands to chin level)*. Now let's close our eyes and remember Jesus, walking on the waves. Let us pray.

Wave-walking Lord,
help us when we're scared.
Say, 'It's me – don't be frightened,'
and hold out your hand.
Amen.

Song

'Be my light when darkness is falling'[58]

---

58. Alison Carver, *30 Catchy New Assembly Songs*, Kevin Mayhew 2009.

Plus

Suggestions for optional extras:

IT Show a picture of a stormy sea.

PROPS A long strip of blue fabric for the front row to wave.

MUSIC 'Be bold, be strong'[59] You could also play Simon and Garfunkel's 'Bridge Over Troubled Water'.

---

59. *Anglican Hymns Old & New*, Kevin Mayhew 2008.

Take Care
The parable of the Good Samaritan

> ## The Plot
> A man is mugged on the way from Jerusalem and left for dead. Two highly religious people – a priest and a Levite – pass him by, but a hated outsider – a Samaritan – stops to help him. He administers first aid, takes him to an inn and pays for his care.
>
> *(Luke 10:25-37)*
>
> ## The Point
> The Samaritan is an example to us all: we should love our neighbours.

Story

Place a chair next to you at the front of the assembly hall.

I've got a story for you today. If you want to hear it, shout, 'What's the story?'

Encourage all to shout: **What's the story?**

This story is known as 'The Good Samaritan' and it's a *parable* Jesus told – in other words, it's a story that makes a point. Even if you don't know the story, you probably have an idea that it's about helping people. If you lend someone a hand today, you might be described as 'a good Samaritan'. But for the Jews who listened to Jesus, this story was a shock. They hated the Samaritans, so 'a good Samaritan' sounded impossible. For us, it would be like hearing about 'a good terrorist'. Let's find out a bit more about the Samaritan and the other characters we'll meet in our story. Can I have four volunteers, please?

Invite four volunteers to come forward and stand at the front. Give them their roles as you introduce them.

Now, this is a Jewish priest from Jesus' time. His special job is to serve God in the Temple in Jerusalem. He wears rich robes and he has to keep himself holy and pure so that he is fit to offer prayers and sacrifices to God. He is a very important man: let's all say politely, 'Good morning, Sir.'

Encourage everyone to say: **Good morning, Sir,** *then ask your priest to give a little nod.*

TAKE CARE – THE PARABLE OF THE GOOD SAMARITAN

You see? He's so important, he won't speak to the likes of us. Next we have a Levite. His tribe was specially chosen by God to be religious leaders. The Levites also have to keep themselves holy and pure, because their job is to serve in God's Temple. He's dressed completely in white and he is an important man, too: let's say, 'Good morning, Sir.'

> *Encourage everyone to say:* **Good morning, Sir**, *then ask your Levite volunteer to reply:* **Good morning.**

He spoke to us! We *are* honoured! Finally, we have a Samaritan. The Samaritans share the same ancestors as the Jews, and some of the same Scriptures, but by Jesus' time the Samaritans were seen as bad, wrong and unclean. *(to the Samaritan)* Are you ready? All these people are going to shout 'Boo!' at you, just because you're a Samaritan. When they do, I want you to turn your back on them, as if you don't care.

> *Encourage everyone to shout:* **BOO!** *The Samaritan turns his/her back.*

Now we know a bit more about three people in our story, let's find out what happened. The events take place on the rocky road from Jerusalem to Jericho. Can you make a path down the middle of the hall like that lonely road?

> *Encourage children to shuffle apart and clear a path down the middle of the hall. Send the Priest, the Levite and the Samaritan to walk along it to the back of the hall.*

This road to the big city twisted through stony hills. It was a dangerous place, because travellers often had money with them, so thieves used to lie in wait by the side of the road. They had plenty of places to hide amongst the rocks, and plenty of heavy stones to throw at people.

> *Introduce your fourth volunteer.*

This man was nervous when he left Jerusalem with gold coins in his pocket and set off down this road. His friends said, 'Take care!' I'm sorry to say he was attacked, robbed and left for dead. So our story begins with a body on the road.

> *Invite your fourth volunteer to lie down and groan at the front of the hall.*

Very religious people in Jesus' time would have looked at this injured man, covered in blood, and thought 'Unclean! Do not touch!' He looks half-dead, and a dead body was seen as unclean. That's what the Priest thought, when he found the body on the road.

> *Encourage the Priest to walk down the path to the front of the hall, look disgusted at the body, walk to the end of the front row and sit down.*

Next came the Levite, thinking about all the important people he had to meet in Jerusalem. He found the body on the road, and he didn't want to touch it, either.

WHAT'S THE STORY?

> *Encourage the Levite to walk down the path to the front of the hall, look disgusted at the body, walk to the end of the front row and sit down.*

Then came the Samaritan, walking along the road by himself. When he saw the man lying on the road, he felt really sorry for him. He went to help him.

> *Encourage the Samaritan to walk down the path to the front of the hall and help the man up.*

He bandaged his cuts and bruises and wiped his face.

> *Encourage the Samaritan to mime this.*

Then the Samaritan helped the man to his feet, gave him a ride on his donkey and took him to a nearby inn. There he made the injured man comfortable.

> *Encourage the Samaritan to help the injured man to the chair.*

The Samaritan said to the innkeeper, 'Here's some money. Please look after this poor man. I'll be back in two days, and you can give me a bill for whatever you've spent on looking after him.'

> *Ask the injured man to sit down and invite the Priest, Levite and Samaritan to stand in a line.*

When Jesus finished telling this story, he asked people a question: 'Which of these three was a neighbour to the injured man?' In other words, who took the best care of this man? Let's vote: hands up if you think that the Priest was the best neighbour.

> *Invite responses.*

Hands up if you think the Levite was the best neighbour.

> *Invite responses.*

And hands up if you think the Samaritan was the best neighbour.

> *Invite responses.*

Of course. The Samaritan, whom everyone hated, turned out to be the kindest, most neighbourly person in the story.

> *Give all your volunteers a round of applause and ask them to sit down.*

TAKE CARE – THE PARABLE OF THE GOOD SAMARITAN

The Point

At the end of this parable, Jesus said to his followers, 'Go and behave like this good Samaritan.' The moral of his story was, 'Love your neighbour as you love yourself'[60] – in other words, take care of other people, look after them and be kind to them, just as you take care of yourself.

The Prayer

For our prayers today, we will ask God to help us be kind to other people. I want you all to cross your arms in front of you, like you're giving yourself a hug, then hold the hands of the people who are sitting next to you.

Encourage everyone to take up this position (as if about to sing 'Auld Lang Syne').

Now that we are hugging ourselves and holding our neighbours' hands, let us pray.

God of Love,
teach us to love ourselves as you love us,
help us to be kind to each other
and show us how to be good friends.
Amen.

Song

'How can I be a good friend today?'[61]

Plus

Suggestions for optional extras:

MUSIC 'When I needed a neighbour'[62]

---

60. Luke 10:27-28
61. Alison Carver, *Sing the day through*, Kevin Mayhew 2009.
62. *Anglican Hymns Old & New*, Kevin Mayhew 2008.

Lost and Found
The parable of the prodigal son

The Plot

A father has two sons. The younger son asks for his inheritance and then goes travelling: in a distant country he wastes all his money on riotous living, then falls on hard times. When he is reduced to working with pigs, he realises he has hit rock bottom. He decides to return home, admit all his wrongdoing to his father and ask for a menial job. He doesn't expect to be treated like a son any more. However, his father welcomes him back with open arms, showers him with gifts and throws a party in his honour. The older stay-at-home brother complains that this is unfair, but the father insists that his lost son's return deserves a celebration. *(Luke 15:11-32)*

The Point

This story shows how God's forgiveness works: his arms are always open in welcome.

Story

I've got a story for you today. If you want to hear it, shout, 'What's the story?'

> *Encourage all to shout:* **What's the story?**

This story is called 'Lost and Found' and it's a *parable* Jesus told – in other words, it's a story that makes a point. It's about a dad who had two sons. Can I have two volunteers to be the brothers, please?

> *Bring forward two volunteers.*

Now, can you put your hand up if your brother or sister is in school with you today?

> *Invite responses, then pick on one or two children and ask them the next question.*

Do you and your brother or sister like doing the same sort of things, or are you quite different?

> *Invite responses.*

The two brothers in our story were very different. The older brother *(select one of your volunteers)* was sensible and good. He always helped out with chores around the house and he always did as he was told. We'll hear more from him later.

LOST AND FOUND – THE PARABLE OF THE PRODIGAL SON

Invite your first volunteer to sit down and bring your second volunteer forward.

But the younger brother was a bit of a wild child. He always wanted to do his own thing, even if it meant getting into trouble. When both the brothers were old enough to leave home, the younger brother said to his father, 'Dad, you know the money you've been saving for me, for when I'm grown-up? Can I have it now?' His dad gave him his share of the money he'd saved – it was a fortune!

Mime giving a big bag of gold coins to your volunteer.

Careful – they're gold coins and they're heavy! Here's all the cash you've ever wanted! What would you do with lots of money like this?

Invite responses.

The younger son went a bit mad with his money.

Encourage your volunteer to move around the assembly hall, miming handing out money, as you continue to tell the story.

He went travelling and everywhere he went, he paid for wild parties, designer clothes and huge feasts. Can you all cheer as if you're all having a great time at one of his parties?

Invite everyone to cheer.

This went on for years. He spent all his money on having fun until there was no more left. Suddenly he found that he was penniless and living in a country where lots of people were hungry. The only job he could find was one that nobody else wanted to do: he had to look after a farmer's pigs. Can you all grunt like pigs?

Encourage grunting and ask your volunteer to mime throwing food at the pigs.

He was so hungry that he was even tempted to eat the pigs' food!

Encourage your volunteer to hold his tummy and look hungry.

At that moment, he remembered how the workers on his dad's farm always got fresh bread, and he made a decision. He would go back home and tell his dad that he was really, really sorry for wasting all his money and doing so many stupid things. He prepared a speech in his head: 'Dad, I'm such a loser. I don't deserve to be your son any more, but please, will you just give me a job on your farm?'

So he went all the way home. His dad was looking out for him and came running down the path to meet him. The son started his speech: 'Dad, I'm such a loser. I don't deserve to be your son any more –' but his dad interrupted him.

WHAT'S THE STORY?

He opened his arms wide for a big hug and said 'My son! You've come home! Here – have these fine new clothes I've been saving for you!' He dressed his son in a rich robe, put a new ring on his finger and sandals on his feet.

Mime dressing your volunteer in these things.

Then the happy father shouted, 'Let's celebrate! He's back! It's party time!'

Encourage everyone to cheer.

However, not everyone was happy. The older brother – remember him? – had been working in the fields all day.

Encourage your first volunteer to stand up again.

How do you think he felt when he saw the party preparations for his long-lost brother?

Invite responses.

The older brother stomped up to his dad and said, 'It's not fair! I've worked hard for you all these years, and I've always done what I was told, but this brother of mine runs away and wastes all his money, and now you welcome him back with a big party! You've never thrown a party for *me*! It's not fair!'

His dad said, 'You're always here with me, and I share everything with you. But we've got to celebrate, because this brother of yours was lost and now he's been found!' The party carried on all night, and everyone celebrated together.

Encourage everyone to cheer.

The Point

This story is known as the parable of the prodigal son: 'prodigal' means careless and wasteful, as the son was when he spent all his money. He knew he'd done lots of stupid things, but his dad forgave him and welcomed him back with lots of presents and a huge party. Jesus told this story to show how God forgives all of us. Whatever we've done wrong, however silly, bad or thoughtless we've been, he is always ready to welcome us with open arms.

The Prayer

We will use two actions for our prayers today. First of all, please hold your arms open as if you are about to give someone a hug. Do it carefully so you don't poke the person sitting next to you!

Encourage everyone to hold out their arms.

LOST AND FOUND – THE PARABLE OF THE PRODIGAL SON

This action reminds us of the father in our story who was ready to welcome his long lost son. Secondly, please wrap your arms around yourself as if you are giving a big hug.

Encourage everyone to make a hugging gesture.

This action reminds us of the big hug which let the son in our story know that he was forgiven and welcomed home. Now watch me as we pray, and join in with these two actions.

Hold out your arms and encourage everyone to do the same.

Forgiving Lord,
thank you that your arms are always open.
Forgive us for the things we have done wrong

Make a hugging gesture and encourage everyone to do the same.

and welcome us home to you.
Amen.

Song

'Father welcomes all his children'[63]

Plus

Suggestions for optional extras:

PROPS A bag of chocolate coins for the Prodigal Son to distribute.

MUSIC 'Come on and celebrate'[64]

---

63. *Anglican Hymns Old & New*, Kevin Mayhew 2008.
64. *Anglican Hymns Old & New*, Kevin Mayhew 2008.

It's Not Fair!
The parable of the workers in the vineyard

The Plot

A farmer hires workers for his grape harvest. Some are hired early in the morning and agree to work for the usual daily wage. Other workers are hired during the day, the last arrivals doing about an hour's work. That evening, everyone gets paid: the last workers are delighted to receive the full daily wage, and the first workers look forward to earning more. They are furious when they receive the same wage, even though they worked all day. They protest and the farmer argues that they got what they were promised, and he is allowed to be generous with his own money

(Matthew 20:1-16)

The Point

God is generous like this: it's his way of doing things.

Story

I've got a story for you today. If you want to hear it, shout, 'What's the story?'

Encourage all to shout: **What's the story?**

This story is called 'It's Not Fair!' and it's a *parable* Jesus told – in other words, it's a story that makes a point. It's about a farmer who owned a vineyard. Who knows what grows in a vineyard?

Invite responses, until you get or give the right answer.

This farmer's vineyard was overflowing with grapes. They were all ripe and they needed picking straight away. So he went to the market place to see if there was anyone who wanted a job. Who'd like to pick some grapes?

Bring forward two volunteers.

He picked two strong workers and said, 'I'll pay you the going rate for a day's work: one denarius each. Deal?' One denarius is worth about £50 in today's money. They shook hands on it.

Shake hands with your volunteers.

IT'S NOT FAIR! – THE PARABLE OF THE WORKERS IN THE VINEYARD

Then he put them to work, telling them to pick as many grapes as they could.

Encourage your volunteers to mime picking grapes.

By nine o'clock, they'd been working for a couple of hours, but there was still plenty more to do. So the farmer went back to the market place and hired two more workers. Who would like a job?

Bring forward two more volunteers.

He promised to pay them a fair wage so they shook hands (*shake hands with your volunteers*) and got on with the job.

Encourage all your volunteers to mime picking grapes.

By midday, the sun was very hot and the workers who'd been slaving away all morning were getting very tired.

Encourage your volunteers to look tired, mop their brows etc.

'Back to work!' said the farmer and went to find more workers. Now who's going to work in the vineyard?

Bring forward two more volunteers, shake hands and set them to work.

Everyone worked really hard, picking as many grapes as they could. At five o'clock, the farmer found some people in the market place who were just hanging around. Who'd like to be the people with nothing to do?

Bring forward two more volunteers.

The farmer asked them 'Why haven't you done anything all day?'
They shrugged and replied, 'No one gave us a job.' So the farmer hired them and put them to work.

Encourage all the volunteers to mime picking more grapes.

At last the harvest was in and the farmer called his workers: 'Time to get paid!' They lined up in order, from the last workers to the first.

Line up your volunteers in order.

He looked at the workers who had loafed around all day and then done an hour's work, and he paid them each a denarius – that's £50 to you and me. They were delighted!

Encourage your volunteers to celebrate.

WHAT'S THE STORY?

The rest of the workers, who had worked up to eleven hours in the hot sun, were excited: they hoped they'd get lots more money! Then the farmer paid them one denarius each, as agreed. They were really cross and shouted, 'It's not fair!'

Encourage your volunteers to look cross and shout: **It's not fair!**

The first two workers said, 'Those lazy layabouts worked for an hour, and we worked in the burning sun all day, and you've paid them the same as us! It's not fair!'

The farmer said, 'Didn't we shake hands and agree on this amount? I've been fair to you, and I've chosen to be kind to the rest. It's my money – why shouldn't I be generous?' The workers went away, some of them feeling fed up and others feeling very happy indeed.

Applaud your volunteers and ask them to sit down.

The Point

How would you feel if you were one of the last grape-pickers, who got a day's pay for an hour's work?

Invite responses.

Hands up if you agree with the first grape-pickers in our story, and you think, 'It's not fair!'

Invite responses.

The people who heard Jesus tell this story were used to picking grapes for local farmers and they didn't think it was fair, either. That's the point. We all expect the last workers in the story to be paid much less than the first workers, because that's fair, but for the farmer, fairness wasn't as important as being generous. He wanted everyone to get the same money. Jesus said God is like the farmer because God's way of doing things isn't always the same as ours. God is good and he loves to give, so whenever we turn to him – whether we arrive first or last – he is ready to welcome us and love us all the same.

The Prayer

Today we'll share a short quiet time as we each say our own prayers in silence. Simply close your eyes and remember whatever or whoever it is you'd like to pray for, then say 'Amen' to finish your prayer. We'll all say it at different times: some prayers might be short and some might be long, but whether you finish praying first or last, God hears all our prayers, just the same. Let us pray.

Pause for a moment of quiet, then say 'Amen' and wait until most people have said it, too.

If you haven't finished yet, you can open your eyes, but keep your prayer going and say 'Amen' in your head when you're ready. God doesn't mind if your prayer goes on all day!

Song

'God is good, God is great'[65]

Plus

Suggestions for optional extras:

- **IT** — Show a picture of some vines loaded with grapes.
- **PROPS** — Some baskets or boxes for collecting the grape harvest; some Monopoly money (£50 notes).
- **MUSIC** — 'God's love is deeper'[66]

---

[65]. *Anglican Hymns Old & New*, Kevin Mayhew 2008.
[66]. *Anglican Hymns Old & New*, Kevin Mayhew 2008.

Seeds, Weeds and Stones
The parable of the sower

The Plot

A farmer sows his crop: some seeds fall on the path and are eaten by birds; some seeds fall on stony ground and grow, then wither in the sun because they haven't put down deep roots. Some seeds grow but are choked by thorns; others fall on good soil and grow into a strong crop which yields a good harvest. *(Matthew 13:1-23)*

The Point

The seeds represent God's word and what happens when people hear it: sometimes they don't understand it – then it's as if God's word has been snatched away from them. Sometimes they accept it joyfully, but their faith doesn't put down roots and it withers at the first sign of trouble. Sometimes God's word is crowded out by the difficulties and temptations of everyday life. But sometimes people hear and understand God's word and it bears fruit in their lives.

Story

I've got a story for you today. If you want to hear it, shout, 'What's the story?'

Encourage all to shout: **What's the story?**

This story is a *parable* Jesus told – in other words, it's a story that makes a point. It's called 'Seeds, Weeds and Stones'. I wonder how many of you are good at growing things. Perhaps you're a member of the school Gardening Club or you help in your garden at home. Do we have some keen gardeners here today?

Invite responses.

If you've ever planted anything, you'll know that sometimes it can be difficult to make things grow: the soil has to be just right, the seeds need enough water and sunlight and even then, not every seed you plant will grow. Victorian farmers used to have a saying about sowing seeds: 'One for the rook, one for the crow, one to let rot and one to grow.' They knew that a good harvest wasn't going to be easy. Jesus told this story about a farmer, and to help me tell it, I'm going to need you to do some actions. First of all, we need some birds. When I say 'BIRDS', I'd like you to flap your hands together like a big black rook or crow. If you like, you can make a noise like a crow, too.

Encourage everyone to make the action and the sound.

When I say 'GREEN SHOOTS', I'd like you to make a little plant grow upwards, using your hand and arm.

Demonstrate this action and encourage everyone to join in, then hold their shoot up.

But these shoots aren't very strong. When I tell you that they WITHER, I want you to make them droop as if they are weak, thirsty plants.

Demonstrate this action and encourage everyone to join in.

Now, there are some stronger plants in our story. When I say 'WEEDS', I'd like you to use both your arms and make them grow up together like tangled weeds.

Move your arms upwards in a twisty, tangling movement and encourage everyone to join in.

Then, last of all, we're going to make a FIELD OF CORN. When I say those words, I'd like you to raise your arms straight up, tall and strong, like ripe corn, and then we'll all wave our arms slowly like a field of corn swaying in the breeze.

Demonstrate this action and encourage everyone to join in.

Now, listen out for the moments in our story when I'll need you to do those actions. Once upon a time, a farmer sowed some seed. He didn't have a tractor: he sowed seed by hand and threw it all over his field.

Mime scattering seed.

Some seeds hit the ground and were stolen by BIRDS.

Everyone flaps their hands and caws like crows.

They swooped down and snatched away the seeds. Now, other seeds landed on stony soil: there was just enough room for them to grow, so they sent out little GREEN SHOOTS.

Everyone stretches up an arm like a green shoot.

Unfortunately, these shoots didn't have room to make strong roots, so when the sun came out, they started to WITHER.

Everyone's arm droops and drops.

Some of the seeds started to grow, but so did the WEEDS.

WHAT'S THE STORY?

Everyone moves both arms upwards in a twisty, tangling movement.

The new plants were choked and crowded out. They had no space or light left to help them grow, so they died.

Everyone lowers their arms.

But some of the seeds took root in good soil. They grew up tall and strong. Stretching towards the sun, they sprouted ears of golden corn. The seeds became a FIELD OF CORN.

Everyone waves their arms like a field of ripe corn.

When the farmer harvested his corn, he had a hundred times more seed than he had at the beginning. It was the best harvest he had ever seen.

Encourage everyone to cheer.

The Point

Jesus explained that everything in this parable meant something. The seed is like God's word, and sowing the seed is like telling people about God. Different things happen when people hear about God. Remember those BIRDS?

Everyone flaps their hands and caws like crows.

Sometimes people don't understand what they hear about God – then it's as if the message has been snatched away from them. Remember the GREEN SHOOTS?

Everyone stretches up an arm like a green shoot.

Sometimes people hear about God and are happy to believe in him, but when things get difficult, their faith WITHERS and fades away.

Everyone's arm droops and drops.

Sometimes people believe in God, but they are so busy worrying or wanting things that God gets crowded out, like a plant choked by WEEDS.

Everyone moves both arms upwards in a twisty, tangling movement.

Finally, do you remember the FIELD OF CORN?

Everyone waves their arms like a field of ripe corn.

Sometimes, people hear about God and believe in him and their faith grows strong. They tell other people about God and they live good lives, showing what his love is like. In this way, the news about God spreads and lots more people believe in him. It's like a great big harvest for God.

Everyone puts their arms down.

SEEDS, WEEDS AND STONES – THE PARABLE OF THE SOWER

So whenever someone tells you about God, there's a chance that a little seed of faith might take root and grow into something amazing.

The Prayer

Today we've been thinking about growing seeds, and our prayer today is for everyone who is still growing. As we pray, we're going to use our hands to make a growing plant.

Demonstrate the following gestures and encourage everyone to join in.

Every plant starts as a seed, *(make a fist)* then it puts out shoots; *(raise your little finger)* then it grows taller and leafier. *(spread all your fingers and stretch up your arm)* We'll use these actions as we pray. Let's begin with a tiny seed.

Everyone makes a fist.

Let us pray.

When we're very small, no one knows who we'll grow up to be.

Everyone raises one little finger.

As we get taller, we discover what makes you, you and me, me.

Everyone spreads their fingers and stretches up their arms.

God, help us grow stronger and wiser and closer to you,
however old we may be.
Amen.

Song

'Push, little seed'[67]

Plus

Suggestions for optional extras:

IT   Time lapse footage of growing plants, for example from David Attenborough's *The Private Life of Plants*.

PROPS   A small bowl of wheat seed (available from health food shops) to show the children.

MUSIC   'So now, it is September'[68]

---

67. *Anglican Hymns Old & New*, Kevin Mayhew 2008.
68. Denis O'Gorman, *Sing the day through*, Kevin Mayhew 2009.

A Tale of Two Sisters
Martha and Mary

The Plot

Jesus and his disciples turn up unexpectedly at the sisters' house in Bethany. Martha runs herself ragged being a good hostess to this horde of guests. Mary sits and listens to Jesus. When Martha complains to Jesus that her sister isn't doing her fair share of the chores, Jesus sympathises but tells her that only one thing is really important, and Mary has made the better choice.

(Luke 10:38-42)

The Point

We need to pay attention to God.

Story

I've got a story for you today. If you want to hear it, shout, 'What's the story?'

Encourage all to shout: **What's the story?**

This story is called 'A Tale of Two Sisters': it's about Martha and Mary. Are there two sisters here today who would like to help me tell this story?

Invite responses and bring forward two sisters (or friends). Ask everyone the following questions.

Before we meet Martha and Mary, I've some questions for you all: who has to help with the chores at home? Who has to help clear away the dishes, wash up or tidy their bedroom?

Invite responses.

Imagine that you're in the middle of tidying your messy bedroom because your mum has told you to, then you come downstairs and find your brother or sister lying on the sofa, reading the Bible. What would you say to your mum?

Invite responses.

Remember that as we tell our story today, because it will help you understand how one of these sisters felt.

A TALE OF TWO SISTERS – MARTHA AND MARY

Introduce your volunteers.

Now, this is Martha. She's the big sister and she lives with her brother, Lazarus, and sister, Mary. Because their parents are dead, Martha's in charge. She's very good at organising things. This is her younger sister, Mary. She's a kind, loving girl who's a bit of a dreamer. Martha and Mary live in a place called Bethany, and one of their best friends is Jesus. Can I have a volunteer to be Jesus, please?

Bring forward a volunteer and stand him to your left.

Jesus never turns up at Bethany alone. He's always surrounded by a crowd of followers – that's all of you.

Indicate everyone in the hall.

One day – SURPRISE! Jesus arrived unexpectedly with a whole group of friends. Here you all are. As always, Jesus was talking to anyone who would listen: he was telling stories, teaching and making people think. His friends loved hearing what he had to say.

Encourage Jesus to gesture as if talking to the assembly hall.

Martha and Mary were delighted to see him. Martha rushed straight to the kitchen, over there, to prepare a special feast for Jesus.

Martha moves to your right. Encourage her to mime busy chopping and cooking actions.

There was so much to do and so many people to feed! But she loved Jesus, so she wanted to make a fuss of him. Martha set about making drinks for everyone, chopping ingredients and cooking tasty treats.

Bring forward Mary to stand with you, in the middle.

Meanwhile, Mary wasn't sure what to do. She knew she ought to go and help Martha in the kitchen – but she loved listening to Jesus and longed to hear what he was saying. Mary made her choice: she sat down with the disciples and concentrated on Jesus.

Send Mary to sit down in front of Jesus and encourage Jesus to hold out his hands as if he's explaining something.

So over there we have Martha, racing around her kitchen and getting more and more stressed. Here we have Mary, listening to Jesus. What do you all think about that?

Invite responses.

Martha didn't think it was fair. She went to Jesus and complained.

Encourage Martha to march over to Jesus.

WHAT'S THE STORY?

Martha said, 'It's not fair! Don't you care that my little sister has left me to do all this work by myself? Tell her to help me!'

But Jesus replied, 'Martha, Martha, you're stressed and you've got a hundred things to think about, but only one thing is really important. Mary's listening to me, and no one's going to stop her: she's made the better choice.'

Now, the Bible story ends there. Let's ask our Martha and Mary what they think. Martha, Jesus said your sister had made the right choice and she didn't have to help you with the chores. How do you feel about that?

Invite Martha's response.

Mary, Jesus said you'd made the right choice when you decided to listen to him. How do you feel about that?

Invite Mary's response, then applaud all your volunteers and ask them to sit down.

The Point

We can all feel sorry for Martha in this story, because we know what it's like to have lots of chores, and we know how unfair it seems when other people aren't helping us. However, Jesus said that it was better to be like Mary, who chose to concentrate on him. This story reminds us that however stressed and busy we might be, nothing is more important than paying attention to God.

The Prayer

One of the best ways of paying attention to God is to pray, and one of the best ways to pray is to stop being busy, like Martha, and simply be still, like Mary. For our prayer today, we're going to use two actions. First of all, when I say, 'BUSY', I'd like you to fold your arms and drum your fingers, as if you're impatient to be doing something. If you like, you can wiggle your toes or tap your feet as well.

Demonstrate this action and encourage everyone else to join in.

Then, when I say, 'STILL', I'd like you to stop wriggling and fidgeting and put your hands together. Sit as still as you can for a moment.

Demonstrate this action and encourage everyone else to join in.

Let us pray.

Lord, you know how BUSY we are.

Fold your arms, wiggle your fingers and tap your toes impatiently.

There's always something for us to do, and we're itching to do it.

Help us every day to be STILL and listen to you.

> *Put your hands together and pause.*

In Jesus' name,
Amen.

Song

'Talk to Jesus every day'[69]

Plus

Suggestions for optional extras:

MUSIC 'To be in your presence'[70]

---

[69]. Barry Hart, *Sing the day through*, Kevin Mayhew 2009.
[70]. *Anglican Hymns Old & New*, Kevin Mayhew 2008.

Dazzled!
The story of Jesus' Transfiguration

The Plot

Jesus takes three disciples up a mountain. There his appearance becomes dazzlingly bright. Elijah and Moses appear next to him, then a cloud covers them all and a heavenly voice declares, 'This is my Son!' Suddenly everything returns to normal, and Jesus swears his disciples to secrecy until after his death. *(Mark 9:2-9)*

The Point

This moment shows that Jesus is the Son of God. He gives his disciples a glimpse of his glory they will never forget.

Story

I've got a story for you today. If you want to hear it, shout, 'What's the story?'

Encourage all to shout: **What's the story?**

This story is called 'Dazzled!' There's an incredibly bright light in it: the Bible says that it's whiter than the whitest washing. Imagine looking at fireworks or a spotlight or the reflection of sunshine on water. Can you all shield your eyes as if you're looking at a dazzling light?

Encourage everyone to do so.

There will be a moment in our story when I'll ask you all to do that, so listen carefully. One day, Jesus called three of his disciples – Peter, James and John. They were some of the first people to follow him, so he knew them and trusted them like old friends. He led them out into the countryside and up into the hills. 'Are we going for a walk?' asked Peter.

'Are we going to pray?' asked James.

'We're not going up that high mountain, are we?' asked John. 'I'm scared of heights!'

They went up the high mountain. Higher and higher they climbed, until they felt as though they were climbing up to heaven. 'Are you going to show us something, Lord?' asked Peter.

'Are we going to meet someone?' asked James.

'Are we nearly there yet?' asked John. Jesus said nothing. At the top, he stood still. His friends thought he was praying, but as they watched, his appearance began to change. At first, his white robes looked even whiter than usual. They started to glow, then they shone with a blinding white light. The disciples were dazzled and they all shielded their eyes.

Encourage everyone to shield their eyes.

As the disciples squinted into the light, they saw two men appear next to Jesus. They recognised them immediately: the man with the long grey beard and two large stone tablets was definitely Moses, the great man who gave their people God's Law. The other man with the long beard was Elijah, who long ago was a great prophet – or spokesman – chosen by God. The disciples were terrified and Peter blurted out the first thing that came into his head: 'Lord! What a good job we came! We can make three special huts – one for you, one for Moses and one for Elijah!'

James said, 'Special huts?'

John said, 'What are you on about?'

Then the bright light began to fade.

Encourage everyone to stop shielding their eyes.

Something even more amazing was happening. A strange cloud came down and covered them all, then a voice from inside the cloud boomed out, 'This is my beloved Son! Listen to him!' Well, the disciples looked at each other in absolute terror: God himself was speaking to them! Suddenly they realised that the cloud had faded away, Moses and Elijah had gone and Jesus was standing there, looking like his ordinary self.

They walked back down the mountain together, and Jesus told his disciples that what had just happened was a secret. They were not allowed to tell anyone until after his death. They reminded each other to keep it quiet: 'Shhh!'

Encourage everyone to put a finger to their lips and say: **Shhh!**

Peter said, 'I won't even tell my brother.'

James said, 'This is just between Jesus and us.'

John said, 'I'm starving! What's for tea?'

The Point

This story about the sudden, dazzling change in Jesus' appearance is called the Transfiguration. When he is changed – or transfigured – like this, Jesus proves to his disciples that he is the Son of God. The dazzling light is a glimpse of God's glory; Moses and Elijah show that Jesus is on the same side as these great men who were chosen by God. Then God himself speaks, just in case anyone has missed the point: 'This is my beloved Son; listen to him!' For the disciples, this is unforgettable proof that Jesus really is who he says he is.

The Prayer

Ask an adult to turn off all the lights in the assembly hall when you give the signal.

The dazzling light in today's story is a reminder that Jesus is sometimes called 'the Light of the world' because he brings the light of God's love into dark places. Those dark places may be fear or loneliness or sadness. For our prayers today, we'll turn the lights off for a moment and pray for anyone we know who is feeling sad, lonely or scared. You might want to pray for yourself, too. Let us pray.

Turn off all the lights.

Jesus, Light of the world,
we pray for everyone who is in a dark place.

Pause, then turn the lights on again.

Shine on us; dazzle us with your light of love, hope and peace.
Amen.

Song

'Light a candle'[71]

Plus

Suggestions for optional extras:

IT Show a visual representation of the Transfiguration (search Google Images).

MUSIC 'Shine, Jesus, shine'[72]

---

71. Val Hawthorne, *30 Catchy New Assembly Songs*, Kevin Mayhew 2009.
72. *Anglican Hymns Old & New*, Kevin Mayhew 2008.

Smelly Feet
Jesus washes his disciples' feet

The Plot

Jesus and his disciples gather together to celebrate the Jewish festival of Passover. Jesus knows he doesn't have much time left before he is arrested and killed, so he washes his disciples' feet. He explains that he is setting them an example of how they should love and serve each other.

(John 13:1-17, 34-35)

The Point

Jesus gives a new commandment: love each other.

Story

Place a chair at the front of the assembly hall.

I've got a story for you today. If you want to hear it, shout, 'What's the story?'

Encourage all to shout: **What's the story?**

This story begins with a custom we might find strange, but which was quite usual in Jesus' time. If a guest arrives at your house, what do you do to make them feel welcome? Do you take their coat? Do you ask them to sit down? What else might you or your parents offer a guest?

Invite responses.

In Jesus' time, guests arrived on foot having walked through dusty fields or along sandy roads. They wore open sandals, so grit and grime got stuck between their toes. One of the kindest things you could say to a guest was, 'Would you like to wash your feet?' Having clean feet again would make them feel comfortable, as if they were at home. Usually, a junior servant was called to wash a guest's feet, using a bowl of water and a towel, and you can imagine what a nasty job it could be. Imagine having to get up close to other people's sweaty toes and verrucas! Today's story is all about foot-washing, which is why it is called 'Smelly Feet'.

This is what happened. Thirteen pairs of hot, dusty feet followed each other through the crowded streets of Jerusalem. Can you stamp your feet as if you're going on a long walk?

Encourage everyone to stamp their feet.

WHAT'S THE STORY?

One foot got trodden on and started to bleed. Can you all make the noise you'd make if someone stepped on your toes?

> *Encourage everyone to say:* **OW!**

Another foot stepped in something squishy that smelt bad. Can you all make the noise you'd make if you stepped in something disgusting on the pavement?

> *Encourage everyone to say:* **YUCK!** *and* **EUUEW!**

Ten feet had blisters; twelve feet had filthy toenails. All twenty-six feet were sweaty and smelly. What would you do if you smelt really smelly feet?

> *Encourage everyone to say:* **PHEW!** *and wave their hands in front of their noses.*

Thirteen pairs of sandals trudged up some stone steps and shuffled into a clean, quiet room where a long table was set for a meal. Jesus and his friends had gathered together to celebrate the Jewish festival of Passover.

Before they sat down, they needed to wash their hands and especially their feet. This was a job for the youngest servant. Can I have a volunteer to be the servant, please?

> *Bring forward a small volunteer.*

I want you to imagine that you're carrying a towel over your arm *(mime placing it there)* and a big bowl of clean water in your hands *(mime handing it over)*. Now, how do you feel about washing thirteen pairs of grown-ups' smelly feet?

> *Invite a response.*

The servant was all ready to wash the men's feet, when something very surprising happened. A pair of hands took the towel from the servant. Can I have a bigger volunteer to play one of the grown-ups in this story?

> *Invite an older child (or a teacher) forward and invite them to mime taking the towel from the servant.*

The hands tied on the towel like an apron and took the bowl full of water.

> *Invite your second volunteer to mime tying the towel around their waist and taking the bowl.*

Those same hands took hold of the first pair of feet. Can I have a volunteer to pretend they're having their feet washed?

> *Invite a volunteer forward and sit them in the chair. Encourage your foot-washer to mime as you describe the actions.*

The hands poured on fresh water and rubbed the feet clean, then dried them gently.

> *The foot-washer mimes washing and drying the volunteer's feet. Then invite your three volunteers to stand together as you name them.*

Those hands belonged to Jesus and those feet belonged to his disciple, Peter. Then Jesus told the rest of the disciples that it was their turn. They were very shocked that Jesus was washing feet like a servant, but he insisted. The servant was more surprised than anyone!

> *Applaud your volunteers and ask them to sit down.*

When all the feet were clean, Jesus explained things to his followers. He said, 'You call me Teacher and Lord, and you're right – but I'm not here to lord it over you. I'm here to serve you by washing your feet. I've done this to show you that you should all do the same – you should wash each other's feet and serve one another. Now I will be leaving you soon, and you won't be coming with me. But I will leave one last thing with you. This is a new commandment: love each other. Love each other, just as I have loved you. That way, people will know that you are my disciples.'

The Point

'Love each other,' said Jesus. 'That way, people will know that you are my disciples.' This is one of the most important rules – or *commandments* – Jesus gave Christians. When he washed his disciples' smelly feet, he showed that loving other people means being kind, helping them, putting yourself out for them and making them feel important. If the Son of God managed to do this, then we can certainly have a go. Whatever we believe in, the world will be a better place if we treat other people in a kind and loving way.

The Prayer

As we think about Jesus washing his disciples' feet, look at the feet of the people sitting near you. Would you wash their feet for them? Would you help them? Will you be kind to them? This is what Jesus was talking about. Let us pray.

Foot-washing Lord,
help us to help each other.
May we learn to love each other
as you loved us.
Amen.

Song

'The world is full of smelly feet'[73]

---

73. *Anglican Hymns Old & New*, Kevin Mayhew 2008.

WHAT'S THE STORY?

> ## Plus
>
> *Suggestions for optional extras:*
>
> **PROPS** You might like to use a large white towel and a large (empty) plastic bowl for the foot-washing props.
>
> **MUSIC** 'How can it be?'[74]

---

74. Becky & Andy Silver, *Sing the day through*, Kevin Mayhew 2009.

Crucify Him!
The story of Good Friday

The Plot

The chief priests want to get rid of Jesus, so they persuade his disciple, Judas, to betray him. Jesus shares a last meal with his friends, then goes into the garden to pray. Judas arrives with soldiers and they arrest Jesus. Interrogation follows, then further betrayal when the crowds are given a choice of prisoners to release: they choose a murderer and Jesus is condemned to die on the cross. He is beaten, tortured and crucified. He dies and his friends bury him in a stone tomb.

(Mark 14:1–15:47)

The Point

Jesus suffered and died for our sins, but this was not the end of his story.

Story

I've got a story for you today. If you want to hear it, shout, 'What's the story?'

Encourage all to shout: **What's the story?**

This story is called 'Crucify Him!' and it's the story of how Jesus died. Apart from Jesus, the most important people in this story aren't the Romans, who nailed Jesus to a cross, or the chief priests, who wanted him dead, or the disciples, who ran away: the most important people are the crowds of ordinary men, women and children who followed Jesus. They have a big part to play in this story, and I'd like you to help me tell it. Will you play the part of the crowds?

Invite responses.

They were a noisy lot, so listen carefully for the things you're going to be shouting.
    When Jesus arrived in Jerusalem, he was a big star. He was more famous and popular than *(name a currently popular band or celebrity)*. Crowds cheered him wherever he went!

Encourage everyone to cheer.

They cheered louder than that!

WHAT'S THE STORY?

Encourage everyone to cheer wildly, then signal for them to stop.

They called Jesus 'God's Chosen One' and they shouted a word of praise: 'HOSANNA!'

Encourage everyone to shout: **HOSANNA!**

The crowds made so much noise that the chief priests worried that Jesus was getting too popular. They thought he was a troublemaker but they couldn't do anything bad to him in front of the crowds, or there would be a riot. They decided to get rid of Jesus quietly.

Put your finger to your lips, encourage everyone to do the same and say: **Shhhh!**

It was the time of the Jewish festival of Passover, when everyone shared a special meal with their family and friends. Jesus and his disciples ate the Passover meal together. His friend, Judas, had secretly agreed to help the chief priests get rid of Jesus; after dinner, he sneaked off to fetch the soldiers. Jesus went out into the garden to pray and there a big gang of soldiers grabbed him. They took him straight to the chief priests, who dragged him to the man in charge: Pilate, the Roman governor. Pilate asked Jesus who he was and what he'd done wrong, and Jesus said – nothing.

All this happened in secret, in the middle of the night. By morning, the crowds were looking for Jesus. They gathered in front of Pilate's grand Roman mansion for the highlight of the festival: every year, they were allowed to choose one prisoner to be released from jail. Pilate appeared in front of the crowds and they all clapped.

Encourage everyone to clap.

He gave them their choice of prisoners: a murderer called Barabbas or Jesus. Now, the chief priests went round telling lies about Jesus and persuading everyone to vote for Barabbas. When Pilate asked, 'Do you want me to release Jesus?' the crowds shouted,
   'NO!'

Encourage everyone to shout: **NO!**

When Pilate asked, 'What do you want me to do with Jesus?' the crowds shouted,
   'CRUCIFY HIM!'

Encourage everyone to shout: **CRUCIFY HIM!**

Pilate was scared of the crowds and didn't want a riot, so he released Barabbas and sent Jesus to be crucified. Soldiers whipped him, dressed him in a crown of thorns and nailed him to a big wooden cross. They put the cross up on a hill for everyone to see. All the crowds *(indicate the assembly hall)* who had cheered and shouted came to watch Jesus die.

Pause for a moment.

When Jesus was dead, his friends wrapped his body in a cloth and buried him in a stone tomb, like a cave. They rolled a big stone across the entrance and left Jesus there.

The Point

Jesus' death on the cross, or *crucifixion*, is the reason why the cross is the Christian symbol. Christians believe that Jesus died for us: he took the punishment for all the bad things we do. He suffered and died in front of crowds of people who all thought that this was The End. But they were wrong: this is just the first part of the Easter story and it finishes with 'To be continued . . .'

The Prayer

When bad things happen, when we're very sad or when somebody we love has died, it can feel as if things are never going to get any better. The really good news of the Easter story is that sadness and death are not the end: there is joy after sadness and life after death. Let us pray.

God of Life,

whenever we are sad or lonely or scared,

remind us that you are with us

and give us hope.

Amen.

Song

'When the day of darkness came'[75]

Plus

Suggestions for optional extras:

MUSIC   'I danced in the morning'[76]

---

75. Val Hawthorne, *Sing the day through*, Kevin Mayhew 2009.
76. *Anglican Hymns Old & New*, Kevin Mayhew 2008.

He's Alive!
The story of Easter Day

> ### The Plot
> Two women called Mary go to Jesus' tomb to anoint his body. There is an earthquake, then an angel rolls the stone away from the entrance and announces that Jesus has risen from the dead. The women leave the empty tomb and meet the risen Christ. They run to tell the disciples the good news of Easter. *(Matthew 28:1-10)*
>
> ### The Point
> Jesus is alive! He is stronger than sin and death.

Story

Place a chair at the front of the assembly hall.

I've got a story for you today. If you want to hear it, shout, 'What's the story?'

Encourage all to shout: **What's the story?**

This story is called 'He's Alive!' but it begins in a graveyard full of dead bodies. I'm going to need some volunteers to help me tell this story. Can I have two soldiers, please?

Bring forward two volunteers.

You are two heavily armed Roman soldiers. Imagine that you've each got a sword in one hand and a shield in the other. But what are two armed guards doing in a graveyard, you may ask? You are guarding this stone tomb: it's like a cave, with a big boulder blocking up the entrance. Can you all imagine a cave here with a big boulder instead of a door?

Indicate the chair next to you.

You two soldiers have your orders: guard this stone tomb. Can you cross your swords in front of it and look fierce?

Encourage the volunteers to take up this position.

HE'S ALIVE! – THE STORY OF EASTER DAY

These soldiers are guarding a dead body: it's Jesus, who died on the cross. The soldiers are there to make sure that his disciples don't steal his body and claim that he's come back to life, as he promised he would. So far, the guards have been here for a day and two nights, and nothing has happened. No one has been near, the stone is still covering the entrance and all is quiet. But what's this? The sun isn't even up yet, and two women are walking through the graveyard. They are both called Mary: can I have two volunteers, please?

Choose two girls sitting at the back of the hall and invite them to stand.

They walk through the dark graveyard, picking their way towards Jesus' grave. Can we make a path for them through the hall?

Encourage everyone to move a little and clear a narrow path through the hall. The girls then walk to the front of the hall.

The guards stand to attention and shout, 'Halt! Who goes there?'

Encourage your guards to shout: **Halt! Who goes there?**

The women stand in front of the grave, ready with spices to rub into Jesus' dead body. The two soldiers bar their way. Suddenly, there is a rumbling and a trembling and a shaking: an earthquake! Can you all stamp your feet to make the sound of an earthquake?

Encourage everyone to stamp their feet.

Then – BAM! – like a streak of white lightning, an angel appears. He shines with bright white light and he is as strong as a superhero. He rolls the stone away and stands on top of it, smiling. Can I have a volunteer to be this powerful angel, please?

Bring forward a volunteer to stand on the chair with arms outstretched.

Imagine that this angel is dazzling to look at: can you all shield your eyes as if you're looking at the sun?

Everyone shields their eyes.

The soldiers are terrified! They drop their swords and run away, shaking.

Ask your soldiers to sit down.

But the angel speaks kindly to the two Marys. 'Don't be scared!' he says. 'I know you're looking for Jesus, who died on the cross. But he's not here: he's come back to life, as he said he would. Look – his grave's empty. He's alive!' Then the angel disappears.

Ask your angel to sit down.

WHAT'S THE STORY?

The two women feel joyfully scared and fearfully happy. They are just about to go and tell the disciples when Jesus himself appears. Can I have a volunteer to be Jesus, please?

> *Choose a volunteer at the back of the hall and invite him to walk through the hall with his arms outstretched.*

Jesus welcomes his two friends. They fall at his feet and worship him.

> *Encourage the two Marys to bow down at Jesus' feet.*

He says, 'Don't be scared. Tell all my friends that I'll see them in Galilee.' With that, he disappears, and the women rush off to find the disciples. The two Marys are the first people to tell the good news of Easter: 'Jesus is alive!'

> *Applaud all your volunteers and ask them to sit down.*

The Point

The stories of Jesus in the Bible are called the Gospels. 'Gospel' means 'good news' and today we've discovered what the good news is: Jesus is alive! Christians believe this means we can all be forgiven for the bad things we do, because Jesus has paid the price on the cross. We can all have life after death because Jesus died and rose again. The good news is that Jesus is still alive and he is stronger than all the bad things in the world, including death.

The Prayer

There is a special word we use particularly at Easter: 'Alleluia!' It means 'Praise God!' and it's like a big, joyful shout. The women who told the good news must have shouted, 'Alleluia!' For our Easter prayer today, we're going to shout this joyful word of praise, and we're going to raise our arms up high as if we're jumping for joy.

> *Hold both your arms straight up, palms facing upwards in a gesture of praise. Encourage everyone else to do the same.*

Hold your arms up like this and when I say, 'We praise you,' I want you all to shout, 'ALLELUIA!' Now, let's put our arms down and practise. 'We praise you:'

> *All raise their arms and shout* **ALLELUIA!** *Repeat if it's not loud enough.*

Now put your arms down and be ready to raise them up and shout. Let us pray.

Thank you, God, for the good news of Easter.
We thank you that Jesus is alive,
and his life gives life to us.
We praise you: *(all)* **ALLELUIA!**
Amen.

Song

'See the baby in the stable'[77]

> **Plus**
>
> *Suggestions for optional extras:*
>
> **IT**　　Show a picture of the stone tomb.
>
> **PROPS**　If you have done a recent project on the Romans, you may have shields and swords to give your volunteer soldiers.
>
> **MUSIC**　'All in an Easter garden'[78]

---

77. Alison Carver, *30 Catchy New Assembly Songs*, Kevin Mayhew 2009.
78. *Anglican Hymns Old & New*, Kevin Mayhew 2008.

I Don't Believe It!
The story of Doubting Thomas

> ### The Plot
> Jesus appears to his disciples after his death. Thomas is absent and when his friends tell him about their visitor, he refuses to believe them: he wants proof. A week later, Jesus appears again, and this time Thomas pokes the wounds left by the crucifixion. He is convinced. Jesus blesses those who believe in him without seeing him. *(John 20:19-29)*
>
> ### The Point
> Believing is hard: we all have doubts, but God never stops loving us.

Story

I've got a story for you today. If you want to hear it, shout, 'What's the story?'

>*Encourage all to shout:* **What's the story?**

This story is called 'I Don't Believe It!' It is a story about believing in God and there are two important lines in it, which I'd like you to help me with. The first line is spoken by people in our story who really believe: 'My Lord and my God!'

>*Encourage everyone to repeat:* **My Lord and my God!**

The second line belongs to people who are finding it hard to believe in God: 'I don't believe it!'

>*Encourage everyone to repeat:* **I don't believe it!**

Now, listen out for your chance to say these two lines in our story. These events happened just after Jesus was killed on the cross. I want you to imagine that we are his friends and disciples and we've all gone into hiding. We're scared that the Romans will kill us, too, so we've locked ourselves in a safe house and we're keeping very quiet.

>*Put your finger to your lips and say 'Shhh!', and encourage everyone else to do the same.*

We're very sad because Jesus, our friend and leader, is dead. Suddenly there's a knock at the door.

I DON'T BELIEVE IT! – THE STORY OF DOUBTING THOMAS

Knock on something wooden.

Oh no! Is it the Romans? Have they come for us, too? Then a voice calls out, 'Let me in! It's me, Mary!' Phew – what a relief. We all know Mary – she was one of Jesus' best friends. We let her in and she blurts out an incredible story about going to Jesus' grave and finding it empty. She says she saw angels and then met Jesus himself! She says he's come back from the dead! She really believes it was him: she says, 'My Lord and my God!'

Some of us believe her and some of us don't. Do you remember the two lines we've learnt? Now is your first chance to use them. You're the disciples and you don't know what to think, so I'm going to divide you. If you've got brown eyes, I'd like you to say 'My Lord and my God!' and if your eyes are any other colour, I'd like you to say, 'I don't believe it!' So Mary has just told you her news and you say:

Encourage everyone to say simultaneously either: **My Lord and my God!** *or:* **I don't believe it!**

Well, we spend all day talking about this extraordinary news. One of the disciples, Thomas, pops out to buy some bread, and the rest of us stay safely behind locked doors, hidden from the Roman soldiers. We're still keeping very quiet.

Put your finger to your lips and say 'Shhh!', and encourage everyone else to do the same.

Suddenly, someone else appears in the room with us. Can I have a volunteer, please?

Invite forward a volunteer to be Jesus (if using face paint, draw red marks on his palms now). He stands with his arms outstretched.

This person has appeared from nowhere. He looks very familiar, and he has sore-looking holes in his hands and feet. It's Jesus!

Encourage your volunteer to shake hands with children in the front row and to show his palms to the rest of the hall.

He shows us the marks where he was nailed to the cross. He encourages us to touch his hands and feel for ourselves that he's real. All of his friends and disciples are convinced that this is Jesus and he's come back from the dead. We all say, 'My Lord and my God!'

Encourage everyone to say: **My Lord and my God!**

Jesus says, 'Peace be with you,' then he disappears.

Encourage your Jesus volunteer to sit down.

WHAT'S THE STORY?

Moments later, Thomas comes back with the bread. Everyone says, 'You should have been here! You've just missed him! We've seen Jesus!'

But Thomas isn't sure. He thinks people are imagining things. He says, 'I don't believe it!'

Encourage everyone to say: **I don't believe it!**

Thomas says, 'Unless I can see him for myself, and unless I can put my finger in the holes left by the nails, I won't believe it's him. I want proof.'

Time passes and the disciples remain in hiding. We're all gathered together like this, with the doors locked, a week later. This time, Thomas is in the room with us when Jesus appears again.

Ask your Jesus volunteer to stand up again.

He says, 'Peace be with you,' then he holds out his hands to Thomas. 'Go on then, Thomas,' he says. Have a good look. Touch my hands; feel the holes where the nails went in. Don't doubt: believe.'

Inspect Jesus' hands yourself.

Thomas holds Jesus' hands and he does believe. He says, 'My Lord and my God!'

Encourage everyone to say: **My Lord and my God!**

Jesus smiles at Thomas and says, 'So now you've seen me, you believe in me, right? If people can believe in me even though they haven't seen me, they're blessed.'

Applaud your Jesus volunteer and ask him to sit down.

The Point

Thomas has become known as 'Doubting Thomas' because he wanted proof, but it isn't really fair to pick on Thomas, because *all* the disciples wanted proof that the visitor really was Jesus: they all had a good look at the wounds that proved he was the same man who died on the cross. This story reminds us that believing in God can be hard – that's why Jesus blessed people who can believe in him without seeing him. We all have doubts and we all want proof, as Thomas and the other disciples did. Their doubts didn't change the fact that Jesus was alive and in the same room. If we have questions or if we're not sure about God, that's OK; nothing changes the fact that he is real and he loves us all.

The Prayer

For our prayers today, I'd like you to join in with the two lines we have learnt today. When I say, 'DOUBT', I'd like you to say, 'I don't believe it!' When I say, 'BELIEVE', I'd like you to say, 'My Lord and my God!'

Practise this once.

We'll begin our prayer with a moment of quiet to tell God about the things we find hard to believe. Let us pray.

God, we bring you our questions
and all the things about you that we're not sure of.

Pause for a brief moment.

Forgive us for the times we DOUBT,
saying, *(all)* **I don't believe it!**
Come close to us so that we may know you and BELIEVE,
saying, *(all)* **My Lord and my God!**
Amen.

Song

'Mary went to mourn for Jesus'[79]

Plus

Suggestions for optional extras:

IT Show a picture of Thomas meeting the risen Christ, for example, 'Still Doubting' by John Granville Gregory, which is a modern painting.

PROPS Use some face paints or a lipstick to make marks on your Jesus volunteer's palms.

MUSIC 'Come into his presence'[80]

---

79. Alison Carver, *Sing the day through*, Kevin Mayhew 2009.
80. *Anglican Hymns Old & New*, Kevin Mayhew 2008.

Come and Have Breakfast!
Jesus appears to the disciples on the beach

The Plot

After Jesus' resurrection, some of the disciples go off for a night's fishing. They catch nothing. At dawn, Jesus appears to them on the beach, but they don't recognise him. He tells them to cast their nets on the other side of the boat and they pull in a bumper catch. They realise it's Jesus and together they share breakfast on the beach.

(John 21:1-14)

The Point

Jesus met ordinary people in ordinary places: we can meet him, too.

Story

I've got a story for you today. If you want to hear it, shout, 'What's the story?'

Encourage all to shout: **What's the story?**

This story is called 'Come and Have Breakfast!' Can you put your hand up if your mum or dad said that to you this morning?

Invite responses.

Can you put your hand up if you said, 'Come and have breakfast!' to a brother or sister, or to your own children?

Invite further responses (including the teachers).

Listen to our story to find out who said these very ordinary words. This story begins on the beach, beside the Sea of Galilee. Jesus' friends were worn out: in the space of a fortnight, they'd been to Jerusalem, watched Jesus die, buried him, gone into hiding and then seen Jesus himself, risen from the dead. After all that, they went back home to Galilee.

'Right, that's it!' said Peter, one evening. 'I'm going fishing!' His old fishing mates, James and John, went with him, and so did some other disciples. They went down to the Sea of Galilee and climbed into the fishing boat that they had used every day, back in the days when they were ordinary fishermen, before they'd become Jesus' disciples. They took their old nets and rowed out into the middle of the lake. There was water all around them, lapping at their boat with gentle waves. I'd like you all to make waves for our story: can you link your hands together in front of you, with your elbows out to the side, and make a gentle, rolling wave movement with your arms?

Demonstrate this action, flexing your hands at the wrist to make the rolling motion. Encourage everyone to join in and continue as you tell the next part of the story.

It was lovely out on the lake at night, surrounded by the peaceful water, but the fishermen didn't catch a thing. Time and again they cast the nets and hauled them in, but there was nothing – not even one little baby fish. As the sun came up, the tired fishermen headed home.

Ask everyone to stop making wave motions.

When they reached shallower water, they saw a stranger on the beach. He shouted, 'No luck with the fishing, then, lads?'

Rather grumpily, they replied, 'No.'

The stranger called out, 'If you throw your nets over the right side of the boat, you'll catch something.' Peter and the disciples looked at each other, wondering what this stranger knew about fish that they didn't, but they cast their nets anyway, as he told them to. Earlier on, you used your hands to make the water; now I'd like you to use your hands to show us what came out of the water in those nets. Fish! More than anyone could believe. Can you wiggle your hands like swimming fish?

Demonstrate this action and encourage everyone to join in.

Look around this hall at all these fish, and imagine them in a net! It was so full, the fishermen couldn't fit it in the boat, so they dragged their catch to shore behind them. Can you pretend that you're dragging in a heavy net full of fish? Hold the ropes in your hands and pull!

Mime pulling and say 'Heave!' Encourage everyone to join in.

At last the bumper catch was safely landed and the fish were flapping and flopping on the sand. Then the disciples recognised the stranger: it was Jesus! He had made a fire and was toasting bread on it. 'Bring us some of those fish you've caught!' he shouted, and he popped them on the fire to cook. When the mouth-watering smell of barbecued fish and fresh toast filled the air, Jesus called to his disciples, 'Come and have breakfast!' Jesus and the fishermen shared a delicious breakfast together, right there on the beach, surrounded by nets and fish.

The Point

Jesus turned up on the beach when the fishermen were doing their ordinary job. He invited them to share his barbecue by saying something we hear almost every day: 'Come and have breakfast!' This story reminds us that church isn't the only place where we can get close to God, and we don't need to use a special, holy language. Like the fishermen on the beach, we can be in a familiar place wearing ordinary clothes and doing everyday things, and God will be with us. He is with us in the school car park, in the supermarket or at home in front of the telly. In today's story, Jesus gave the fishermen a miraculous number of fish; who knows what amazing things he might do in our lives?

The Prayer

For our prayer today, I'd like you to close your eyes and listen to these words. Make them your own prayer by joining in with 'Amen' at the end. Let us pray.

Lord Jesus,
you said to your disciples, 'Come and have breakfast.'
When we eat our Weetabix, or Shreddies, or Coco Pops, or toast,
and when we drink our milk, or juice, or tea, or coffee,
help us to remember that you're with us
at the start of another ordinary day.
Amen.

Song

'It's good to pray'[81]

Plus

Suggestions for optional extras:

IT Show a picture of the shores of Lake Galilee or a close-up of lots of fish in a net.

MUSIC 'Each morning of the week'[82]

---

81. Val Hawthorne, *30 Catchy New Assembly Songs*, Kevin Mayhew 2009.
82. Alison Carver, *Sing the day through*, Kevin Mayhew 2009.

Goodbye
Jesus ascends into heaven

The Plot

Forty days after Jesus' resurrection, he promises the disciples that they will receive the power of the Holy Spirit and he tells them to be his witnesses all over the world. Then he is lifted up into the sky. Two angels tell the disciples that Jesus has gone home to be with his Father in heaven, and that one day he'll come back again.

(Acts 1:1-11)

The Point

This event is called the Ascension and it's the last time the disciples see Jesus. He promises them the Holy Spirit and tells them to spread the good news about him. This promise is fulfilled at Pentecost and Christians believe that it's their job to tell people about Jesus.

Story

Before you begin, quietly invite two children in the front row to be angels at the end of the story. Tell them to stand up and spread their arms like wings when you tap them on the head.

I've got a story for you today. If you want to hear it, shout, 'What's the story?'

Encourage all to shout: **What's the story?**

This story is called 'Goodbye'. You'll remember that Jesus' friends said goodbye to him on Good Friday, when he died on the cross. Then he came back from the dead and appeared to them many times. Finally, forty days after Easter, they said goodbye for the last time. This is what happened.

Jesus gathered his disciples together and got ready to say goodbye. Can I have a volunteer to be Jesus, please?

Bring forward your volunteer and stand him at the front, then indicate everyone else in the hall.

WHAT'S THE STORY?

All of you are Jesus' friends and disciples. You're ready to listen to him. First of all, Jesus told his disciples what to do. He said, 'Don't leave Jerusalem. Wait here for God's promise. Do you remember how John the Baptist baptised people with water? All of you got soaked in the river. Well, in a few days you'll be baptised with the Holy Spirit. You'll be drenched in God's power.'

> *Pick out individuals as you say each of the following lines.*

One disciple said, 'What sort of power?'

Another disciple said, 'Do you mean, like a superpower?'

A third disciple said, 'God's power – for me? WOW!'

Jesus smiled and said, 'God will send you the power of his Holy Spirit very soon.'

A fourth disciple asked, 'Lord, what about our nation? When will you give Israel back her power?'

Jesus replied, 'That's up to God. He's in charge. But *you* will have power when the Holy Spirit arrives, and *you* will be my witnesses: you'll tell people about me here in Jerusalem, throughout the Middle East and all over the world.' There was a pause while all Jesus' friends and disciples thought about this. They wondered how they would ever be brave enough to tell the world about Jesus.

> *Pause briefly.*

Suddenly, an extraordinary thing happened! As the disciples looked at Jesus, he was lifted up into the sky, higher and higher, until clouds hid him from sight. I want you to imagine that our volunteer is being lifted up higher than this hall, up into the clouds until he disappears from view.

> *Point at a space just above your volunteer's head and, as he sits down, raise your hand gradually higher until you are pointing at the ceiling.*

Look up and imagine that you are the disciples peering right up into the clouds, wondering where Jesus has gone. Imagine that you're shielding your eyes from the sun as you squint into the sky.

> *Shield your eyes and look at the ceiling, encouraging everyone else to do the same. When everyone is craning their necks upwards, tap your angel volunteers on the head so that they come and stand next to you with their arms outstretched.*

Suddenly, a soft voice said, 'Men of Galilee!'

> *Call everyone's attention back to you and the angels.*

Two angels in shining white robes had appeared from nowhere. They said gently, 'Men of Galilee, why are you looking into the sky? Jesus has gone home. He's been taken up into heaven, and one day he will come back in the same way.'

> *Applaud all your volunteers and ask the angels to sit down.*

GOODBYE – JESUS ASCENDS INTO HEAVEN

The Point

This miraculous event is called the Ascension because it's about Jesus going up – or *ascending* – into heaven, where he lives for ever. It was the last time the disciples saw Jesus, but there are two more reasons why it's important: Jesus made a promise and he gave his disciples a job to do. He promised them the power of God's Holy Spirit and told them to spread the good news about him. Christians still believe that it's their job to tell people about Jesus. As for that mysterious power, we'll find out more about it in our next story . . .

The Prayer

As we remember the Ascension, when Jesus went up into the sky, we think about the disciples looking up. We very often think of God and heaven as being 'up there', but we can also think of God as being 'all around', because he is always with us, and we can think of him as being 'in our hearts', because there is goodness and love in all of us. We're going to use these three places in our prayer this morning: 'up there', 'all around' and 'in our hearts'. I'd like you to join in with an action for each one. When I say, 'UP THERE', I'd like you to point straight upwards as if you know the answer to your teacher's question.

> *Demonstrate raising your hand and pointing and encourage everyone else to join in.*

When I say, 'ALL AROUND', I'd like you to move your head and look all around the hall.

> *Demonstrate this action and encourage everyone else to join in.*

And when I say, 'IN OUR HEARTS', I'd like you to cross your hands over your heart.

> *Demonstrate this action and encourage everyone else to join in.*

Now, let's add all these actions to our prayer. Let us pray.

God in heaven,
sometimes we think of you as UP THERE,
but you are with us and you are ALL AROUND.
Help us to find you IN OUR HEARTS
so that we might love each other
as you love us.
Amen.

Song

'When I look into the sky'[83]

---

83. Val Hawthorne, *30 Catchy New Assembly Songs*, Kevin Mayhew 2009.

WHAT'S THE STORY?

> **Plus**
>
> *Suggestions for optional extras:*
>
> **MUSIC**   'He is Lord'[84]

---

[84]. *Anglican Hymns Old & New*, Kevin Mayhew 2008.

Wind and Fire
The story of Pentecost, the Church's birthday

The Plot

In Jerusalem, the disciples are in hiding during the Jewish festival of Pentecost. Suddenly they are visited by a strong wind, then flames appear above their heads. It is the Holy Spirit and they are filled with his power. They rush into the streets, shouting the good news about Jesus. Miraculously, they have the power to speak in many different languages, so that every foreign visitor understands them. Thousands of Jewish pilgrims are converted that day and the number of believers steadily increases.

(Acts 2)

The Point

Pentecost reveals the power of the Holy Spirit and it is the Church's birthday.

Story

I've got a story for you today. If you want to hear it, shout, 'What's the story?'

Encourage all to shout: **What's the story?**

This story is called 'Wind and Fire'. Some very dramatic events happen in it and I'd like you to do the special effects for me. First of all, there is a strong wind, like the wind that warns you a hurricane's coming. Can you puff out your cheeks and make the noise of a wild wind?

Encourage everyone to make loud 'whooshing' sounds.

The second special effect we need is fire. I'd like you to make tall, flickering flames, like this:

Raise your arms above your head in a snaking movement and encourage everyone to join in.

Listen out for the wind and the fire in our story. Now, I'd like you to imagine that you are all Jesus' disciples. You're hiding in a locked room in Jerusalem because you don't want the Roman soldiers to get you. They killed Jesus on the cross, but you know that Jesus has come back from the dead. He has visited you several times. A few days ago, you saw him go back up into heaven. The soldiers are waiting to arrest anyone who so much as mentions the words 'Jesus' and 'God' in the same

WHAT'S THE STORY?

sentence, and that's why you're in hiding. The door is locked and bolted, so you're safe for now. You're waiting together for Jesus to keep his last promise: he said that he'd send you God's special power – the power of the Holy Spirit. None of you really knows what that is.

> ***Pick out individuals as you say the next few lines.***

The power of the Holy Spirit? You wonder if it will be a kind of superpower. You wonder if it means you'll rule the world. You wonder if it's going to hurt. All of you sit together, wondering and waiting behind locked doors.

But what's happening now? There's a powerful wind rushing inside this place! It's filling the whole house!

> ***Encourage everyone to make the sound of the wind.***

It's getting stronger and stronger . . .

> ***Encourage everyone to make the sound of a hurricane.***

Then: guess what? Jesus' best friend, Peter, has got fire coming out of the top of his head – but it doesn't burn him at all. The fire catches each of you in turn, until you all look as if you're wearing tall crowns made of flames.

> ***Encourage everyone to move their arms above their heads like flames, then put their arms down.***

Now you all feel very different. You feel full of strength and power.

> ***Encourage everyone to sit up straight and confidently.***

Suddenly, you can't wait to tell people about Jesus! You want to shout his name from street corners! Let's have twelve volunteers to represent us all.

> ***Bring forward twelve volunteers.***

Here are the twelve disciples: they've breathed in the powerful wind that blew through their house, and they've felt strange fire burning above their heads. Now they feel bolder and stronger than they've ever felt before. They have been filled with God's Holy Spirit. *(to the volunteers)* Can you look bold and strong, as if nothing and no one could ever frighten you again?

> ***Encourage your volunteers to stand boldly, then address the rest of the hall.***

Now the rest of you have a different part to play: you are a crowd of ordinary people in Jerusalem. You are tourists and pilgrims, visiting the city for the Jewish festival of Pentecost. You come from all over the world.

WIND AND FIRE – THE STORY OF PENTECOST, THE CHURCH'S BIRTHDAY

Pick out individuals and groups at random as you say the next few lines.

You're from Rome and you're from Egypt; some of you are from Arabia, some from Libya, some from Greece, some from Asia, some from Judea and the rest of you from more places besides. You all speak your own languages.

Turn back to the disciples.

Now, disciples: you lot are from Galilee. None of you even knows how to count up to ten in French, but you open your mouths and shout out a message for everyone to hear: 'Jesus is God!'

Encourage the disciples to shout: **Jesus is God!**

Suddenly you find yourselves speaking in loads of different languages, telling people about Jesus in words that everyone here can understand! Surely, that's impossible – no one has ever seen or heard anything like it! A family from Greece hears you speaking Greek and a woman from Rome hears you speaking Latin. When you say, 'Who wants to be on Jesus' side?' thousands of people reply, 'Me!' Can we all put our hands up, as if we're all volunteering?

Encourage everyone in the hall to put their hands up.

That's what happened when the disciples said, 'Who wants to be on Jesus' side?' Three thousand people were baptised, and that was when the Church began. Everything that we now know as the Church was kick-started by God's Holy Spirit. That special day – Pentecost – was the Church's birthday.

Applaud your volunteers and ask them to sit down.

The Point

The star of today's story was that mysterious power, God's Holy Spirit. He appeared like wind and fire, then spread the good news about Jesus like wildfire: the disciples told the tourists and pilgrims, then the tourists and pilgrims took the news home with them to their own countries. As more and more people believed in Jesus, they became a group of believers with Jesus in common: this group is what we now call the Church. Christians celebrate Pentecost because it is the Church's birthday.

The Prayer

At Pentecost, we remember God's Holy Spirit who filled the disciples with his power and made them strong. We will pray for God's Holy Spirit to help us when we are feeling weak, scared or useless. In our prayers, we'll use our breathing, because the Bible often describes the Holy Spirit as wind or breath. When I say, 'BREATHE', I'd like you to take a big, deep breath, then let it out slowly as we pause to pray. Are you ready? Let us pray.

Holy Spirit, BREATHE into our lives.

WHAT'S THE STORY?

Take a deep breath and let it out slowly, encouraging everyone else to do the same.

Breath of God, BREATHE on us;

Take a deep breath and let it out slowly, encouraging everyone else to do the same.

Spirit of Pentecost, may you BREATHE into us your strength and power.

Take a deep breath and let it out slowly, encouraging everyone else to do the same.

Amen.

Song

'All over the world'[85]

Plus

Suggestions for optional extras:

- **IT** — A close-up picture or video footage of fire.
- **PROPS** — If yours is a Church school, you could have a cake with candles to celebrate the Church's birthday. Invite a volunteer to blow out the candles.
- **MUSIC** — 'Colours of day'[86]. You might also like to invite everyone to sing 'Happy Birthday' to the Church.

---

85. *Anglican Hymns Old & New*, Kevin Mayhew 2008.
86. *Anglican Hymns Old & New*, Kevin Mayhew 2008.